P9-EDD-610

WITHDRAWN

Vital Concepts of The Bible

220.08
M 199

VITAL
CONCEPTS
of
THE BIBLE

by

John L. McKenzie, S.J.

81984

DIMENSION BOOKS
WILKES-BARRE ‹› *PENNSYLVANIA*

LIBRARY ST. MARY'S COLLEGE

First American Edition
Published by Dimension Books
Wilkes-Barre, Pa.

Library of Congress Catalog Number 67-19969

Grateful acknowledgment is hereby made to *The Commonweal*, *The Way*, *The Proceedings* of The North American Liturgical Conference, and *The Month* for permission to reprint in this book in revised form articles which originally appeared in those publications. Arrangement of the articles, revision and general title suggested by the Publisher.

Copyright © 1967 by John L. McKenzie

Nihil Obstat
   Rt. Rev. Msgr. James T. Clark
   Censor Librorum
   February 14, 1967

Imprimatur
   ✠ J. Carroll McCormick
   Bishop of Scranton
   February 15, 1967

Contents

Contents

Into The Desert

JERUSALEM has become a large city, and in spite of the medieval quaintness of the walled town, a modern city. Yet, for all the devastations Jerusalem has suffered in its thirty-five hundred years of recorded history, the roots of its past impress themselves upon the observer with a sharpness which he experiences in few other places where man dwells. The impression does not come from the ruins of ancient Jerusalem, for they are few and poor and entirely without the magic of the Acropolis of Athens or the colonnades of Palmyra; it comes from the situation of Jerusalem in a landscape which has changed less with the passage of years than the city has changed, a landscape which at once seems familiar to anyone who has read his Bible with assiduity. When one ascends to the top of Jerusalem's towers or to the summit of its neighboring hills, one is within sight of the desert, and one knows why the desert is mentioned so many times in the Bible.

The Israelites could never forget that they had been a desert people, and indeed many of them remained desert people; did one see nomads less frequently near the Israelite cities of Solomon and Ahaz than one sees them in the neighborhood of the Jerusalem of Hussein? One need not travel many miles from Jerusalem to lose oneself "in a desert land, in a howling wilderness of waste."[1] But this is only the fringe of the desert wastes of Syria and Arabia, which seem to stretch into infinity. To stand at the threshold of these wastes sobers one's thoughts.

Ernest Renan said that monotheism was born between the twin vastnesses of the desert floor and the desert sky. Between these two vastnesses man sees nothing but himself, and he becomes aware of the "Thou" voicelessly making its presence felt to his own "I." Historians of religion have generally and wisely decided that this theory is nonsense. Man is no more perceptive of the divine reality in the desert than he is in other vast empty spaces, which Renan would have done well to explore, at least by voyaging in books. The desert impresses one no

[1] Deut 31,10.

10

more with its cosmic emptiness than do the Arctic wastes; but the Eskimo has not been an evangelist of monotheism to the world. The experience of the desert is no more mystical than the experience of the dark grey terror of the North Atlantic, or of a wind-swept mountain peak buried in its perennial snow, or even of the broad sky seen from 30,000 feet in the air from the cabin of a modern airplane. All these elemental scenes have something in common, and that something is not an awareness that God is near; it is an awareness that death is near, which is not quite the same thing. One realizes that these vast empty spaces are empty because they reject man; they are actively, murderously hostile. The desert will kill you unless you have the skill and the deter-mination to outfight it and outwit it. It is always something of a shock in a country which is well-equipped with the conveniences which sustain and protect the traveller, when one reads annually of some unwary tourists in, say the western states of the U.S.A., who perish in the desert as people per-ished a hundred years ago when they crossed the desert in prairie schooners. These unfortunate people do not realize that when they explore the desert they flirt with death.

This is the fatal charm of the desert, its challenge. In the desert the complexity of civilization vanishes as if it had never existed; one realizes how little of the surface of the globe is available for human life, and one feels that one is an intruder. Life is reduced to a very few simple decisions, and a wrong decision may be fatal. One cannot allow oneself to be distracted from the single purpose, which is survival; and unless one accepts the fact that survival in the desert is totally demanding, one will not survive. The desert, like the Arctic waste, the mountain peaks, the ocean, and the wild blue yonder of the air, is home only to those few who have mastered the highly specialized skills which survival in these elements demands, and who have the will to live to an unusual degree.

Reflection, I think, shows that the desert does not produce the awareness of God as much as it produces the awareness of evil. Those who survive in the desert do so because they know that they are never out of the grip of a malignant force which seeks their lives. They do not pretend that they live in a world where all is right. Where water is very properly and literally life, water ranks among the destructive agents which maintain the desert in its hideous ragged erosion. Rainfall is an event which may happen no more than half a dozen times in a year, and one cannot watch a thunderstorm approaching without knowing why Psalm 28 is written as it is.[1] It is not the gentle friendly rainfall for which the Church prays and for which the farmer thanks God, and it would never be compared by the desert poet to mercy. The desert dweller runs for shelter, not because he is afraid of getting wet nor because he knows anything of positive and negative charges, but because he has learned that in that empty landscape a man is easily the tallest projection in sight, and he is a sure target for what all desert people call the bolt, the hammer, or the arrow of God. The rain falls in torrents and tears through the ground like a giant harrow, leaving ugly barren furrows where the rock crops to the surface. No, even the forces which

[1] "The voice of the Lord flashes like flames of fire. The voice of the Lord shakes the wilderness, the Lord shakes the wilderness of Kadesh." Ps 28, 7-8.

13

man thinks are friendly turn against him in the desert. But while the rare desert thunderstorm is more terrifying, is it any more menacing than the incredibly hot wind which blows from the very heart of the desert, dehydrating and debilitating the desert dweller or, at its worst, blinding him in a whirlwind of sand and obliterating tracks and traces? Then even the nomad whose element is the desert may be lost; and one who is lost in the desert is usually lost forever. The desert is not the place which breeds optimism; the nomad knows, and all who share his life must learn, that there are genuine evil forces which can be mastered only by decision and persistence; one who refuses to admit their reality or discounts their power has already lost the battle with them.

No one can do anything but fear the desert once he has sensed its raw violence. This is perhaps another feature of its fascination, its candor; it is honestly what it is and pretends to be nothing else. It is murderous and unforgiving, but it does not deceive. There is a certain attraction in its naked and undisguised malignancy, which is present even when for a few minutes during early morning and late afternoon hours it is transformed into a paradise of flashing color. It can mantle itself after the rains in lovely patterns of wild flowers, which it seems to delight in withering: "the flower of the field which blossoms today and tomorrow is cast into the oven." For the desert is death, and it will not tolerate life.

Surely if man were to form his idea of God from his desert experience the god so conceived would be created in the image and likeness of the desert. He would be an unforgiving enemy, harsh and cruel. He would in fact be not unlike the Mesopotamian Nergal, who seems to exhibit the character of the murderous burning sun, or of the Syrian Hadad, a stormy warrior who flings his thunderbolts with awesome abandon. The God of Israel was not a reflection of the desert; yet the desert was the scene where man in the Old Testament encountered God. No one who is at all familiar with the Old Testament can think that the God whom Israel encountered in the desert derived His character from the desert; if He had, no Israelite poet could ever have said that His covenant of love is above all His works.

Such a God could have claimed only that terrified submission which man must pay to superior irrational force. The desert imposes a code of life, but it is not the code which Israel attributed to Yahweh. Israel's encounter with Yahweh in the desert introduces us to the desert as a way of life; for it is a way of life and not merely a phenomenon of nature.

The civilization of Mesopotamia and Canaan of the second millennium B.C. was advanced in more ways than we can easily realize. Its cities were rich and prosperous, its commerce flourished, its agriculture supported large populations. The nomad looks at civilization with a mixture of envy and contempt: envy for its riches in comparison with his own existence on the margin of starvation, contempt for the toil and the loss of liberty which is the price civilized man pays for his security. More than this, ancient civilized man in Egypt and Mesopotamia and Canaan worshipped the gods which gave him the goods which he most anxiously desired; the civilization was frankly and grossly materialistic, and its gods were modelled to suit its own ideals. To the Israelite these were false gods which promised spurious goods. Civilized man could never find God in his cities because he never sought God there. To find God man must leave the petty avarice of the cities behind him and go into the desert where the issues, as we have observed, were reduced to a few simple decisions on which life and death depended. In the desert one could see much more clearly what the basic values are; one could not afford to neglect the difference between what is vital and what is not.

I do not mean to suggest by these reflections that I am proposing in a more subtle form the discredited theory of Renan. It is true, nevertheless, that even a revealed religion is conceived by any people in the dominant ideas of its own cultures. There were differences between Greek and Latin Christianity in the early centuries of the Church, just as there are differences slowly emerging at the present time between European Christianity and the Christianity of the Far East. Members of what is a single family of nations in Europe think they detect differences between the churches of Anglo-Saxon, Germanic, and Latin countries. It is extremely difficult to imagine anything like the Neapolitan festival of San Gennaro being celebrated in Brompton Oratory, London. When Israel encountered Yahweh it was not a settled people, and its thoughts and ways were those of the desert. After Israel became a settled people in Canaan, their conception of their God was enlarged; after all, civilized man must find God too, and he has neither then nor now decided that he must choose between God and civilization. Israel always knew which choice it would have to make if the choice were put in these ultimate terms. This is the hard choice of the desert which reduces everything to the rigid alternatives of life and death; it is not a place of compromise. The desert encounter with Yahweh left a lasting impression on the religious belief of Israel long after Israel had become a settled people. But as we have noticed, in the land of Israel one is never far from the desert.

The first and classic encounter of God and man in the desert occurs in the vision of Moses.[1] Through the dialogue of this story runs a single theme: the imperious will of Yahweh to deliver His people. The theme is heightened by contrast with the reluctance of Moses to accept the saving will of Yahweh,

---

[1] Exod 3.

18

which is not hard to understand; the deliverance of
Israel meant a challenge to the Egypt of the Nine-
teenth Dynasty, a powerful kingdom. But in the
desert there is no room for compromise; one makes
the necessary decision to live, or one dies, and Israel
could live only by the saving will of Yahweh.

Israel, led by Moses, must journey into the desert
to find the God in whose name Moses spoke. Moses
encountered Him in the burning bush, and Israel encountered Him at Sinai.[2] The desert, we have noticed, reveals nature in its harsh cruelty; the Sinai
traditions of Israel show a deep awareness of the
harshness of the scene. An old tradition, but not
nearly as old as Israel, has placed this unique meeting in the Sinai peninsula, which is raw and harsh
enough to suit anyone's taste; whether this location
is correct or not is of little importance, for any number of desert sites are just as harsh. We are not
here attempting to derive Israel's awareness of God
from its awareness of the desert; but it is again
worth our notice that in an atmosphere such as that
of Sinai, Israel could not run and hide from Yahweh
as it could do in the fields of Egypt and the cities of

---

[2] Exod 19.

19

Canaan. In the desert there is no place to which one can run; Israel was, once again, brought face to face with a decision to live or to die, and there was no way to evade it. Yahweh, the lord of the desert, could leave them to perish if they did not accept His saving will. Their deliverance and their survival could be achieved only through the means which He placed before them: a total submission to His will. Yahweh is a desert God in the sense that Israel must accept Him on His own terms if it is to live. The covenant which was its life was formed in the desert.

The desert in Israelite tradition was a place of testing. Modern novelists and playwrights are fond of situations in which the civilized man, suddenly snatched from his artificial climate, his police and fire protection, his easy transportation and the security of his regular routine, must vanquish raw nature with nothing but his bare hands and his wits. In the minds of most of our writers of fiction this is perhaps the only true test of the quality of a man; and many of them seem convinced that the men who succeed best in the forum and the market would fail most miserably in a test with the elements. There is some truth in the conception of The Admirable Crichton. The qualities which keep the Eskimo alive in the Arctic and the Bedawi alive in the desert are not the qualities which would protect him in the streets of London or New York; and the bright young men of Madison Avenue would starve in the desert. The Bedawi, as we have observed, can never forget that survival demands a total dedication; the citizen of New York or London does not conceive his existence in these terms. Whether one test proves more than another is not at the moment relevant nor need it be decided; but it is of interest to note that the Old Testament view of the desert as a place where a man or a people is tested is by no means peculiarly biblical.

It is, however, peculiarly biblical to think of the desert as a place where God is tested; we read this each day in Psalm 94, which stands at the beginning of the divine office.[1] The Israelites explained the old name Massah which stood in their desert tradi-

---

[1] 'Harden not your hearts, as at Meriba, as on the day at Massah in the wilderness, When your fathers tested me, and put me to the proof, though they had seen my work'. Ps 94,8-9.

tions as a place where Israel tested Yahweh.[2] But the desert was also a place where Yahweh tested Israel.[3] Anyone who has travelled in a group knows that nothing tests the members of the group like this shared experience; and it is an even more searching test when travel becomes a race with Death. So Yahweh and Israel journeyed through the desert, Yahweh testing Israel's fidelity to the promise which it had given and Israel testing Yahweh by stretching His patience, so to speak, to the limit. Israel failed the test, both in obedience and in faith in the power of Yahweh to execute His will to save; and the second failure was more fundamental than the first. Obedience must rest ultimately upon faith in the leadership of him who leads.

Yet while the desert is unforgiving, Yahweh is not. When faith fails and hope is shattered, He alone endures; and Israel recognized that it survived its desert experience because He had carried it in His arms as a man carries his child.[1] The speaker could have added that He carried a wilful and rebellious child. This was the test of Yahweh which

---

[2] Exod 17,7. [3] Exod 15,25; Deut 8,2. [1] Deut 1,31.

revealed His character more clearly than anything else in the experience of Israel. He is proved not only lord of nature, lord of history, king of Israel, but he is proved superior to the mere human level of feeling and decision. When a prophet wished to remind Israel of the fidelity of Yahweh to His word, he appealed to the passage of Israel through the desert.[2] God, as well as man, is proved in human tribulation.

There is a story of Elijah who, fortified by heavenly bread, walked forty days and forty nights to the mountain of God, Horeb, as the mountain is called in some traditions.[3] It is obvious that when this story was told its tellers had no idea of where Horeb might be, except that it was a great distance. But it was the place where Israel had met Yahweh, and it was the place where Elijah went to search for Him; for Elijah was sure that He could no longer be found in Israel, where all faith in Him seemed to have disappeared. Israel had surrendered to Canaanite civilization; it aped the manners and ways of Canaan, and now it worshipped the gods of Canaan. So Elijah thought; and he hoped to find Yahweh where

---

[2] Jer 2,6.   [3] I Kg 19.

Yahweh had first revealed Himself to Israel and there lay down his life, because Yahweh and Israel had parted. He found Yahweh; but his discovery seems to be a deliberate inversion of the theophany of Sinai. For the elements are in convulsion, as they were in the story of Sinai; but Yahweh was not in the wind nor the earthquake nor the lightning. He is present in a barely perceptible movement of the air; and He assures Elijah that He is still the God of Israel, even when He does not manifest Himself in the convulsions of nature.

Elijah was only the first in a long line of men who have returned to the desert in hope of a new vision of God by which they might restore their faith and their courage. God was no more in Horeb than in Israel, but Elijah had to return to the desert in order to learn this. There, with the complexity of civilization far behind him, the basic truths came more clearly into view. The desert where the religion of Israel was born is the source whence it draws its strength for renewal.

It was perhaps a hundred years or so after Elijah that another prophet looked at his people Israel and saw that they were still unfaithful to Yahweh. Hosea's conception of Israel, in the opinion of almost all exegetes, was formed in the light of a searing personal experience: the infidelity of his own wife. He is the first to perceive and to express in the relations of man and God the theme of rejected love. Israel sells its heart for wool and flax, grain and wine and oil, gold and silver. These she finds more desirable than the love of Yahweh, and she gives her love to the gods who promise her these things. She has become candidly mercenary. How does one reach the heart of such a person, when there seems to be no heart to reach?

Hosea sees only one possibility for the spiritual regeneration of Israel, and that is a return to the desert.[1] He idealizes the traditions of the exodus and the wandering and represents them as a time of Israel's youthful affection and loyalty to Yahweh. The history was more complicated than this, but the Old Testament takes a simple view of things; in the period of the desert Israel was still a people of the desert and had not yet been seduced by the worldliness of Canaan. Perhaps, if Israel is taken back

---

[1] Hos 2,14.

to the harsh reality of the desert and deprived of the wealth and luxuries of Canaan, she will recognize once again the spouse of her youth. For the desert is a place where life is reduced to a few vital decisions. It can be for Israel, as it was for Elijah, a place where faith and courage are restored. Israel met Yahweh there for the first time, and she will see Him more clearly if she returns to the desert. With no other noise to distract the attention, Yahweh can "speak to her heart." The desert is hideous and cruel, with death stalking those who enter it; but for one in Israel's desperate condition it can be a door of hope.[2]

It is, then, not surprising that the Gospel begins with "the word of the Lord which came to John the son of Zachary· in the desert."[3] John came not only in the spirit and power of Elijah,[4] but also in Elijah's garments and way of life. Elijah of Tishbe in Gilead, wherever this may have been, never appears in the stories of the books of Kings as a man with a fixed abode; and John dwells "in the desert" subsisting on the meager diet which the desert offers. The king-

---

[2]   Hos 2,15.   [3]   Lk 3,2; Mt 3,1.   [4]   Lk 1,13.

dom of God is announced from the desert by a man whose life and manner affirm the austere rigor of the desert. His person, like his message, is an antithesis to the ideals of his contemporaries. John announced the greatest crisis in the history of Israel, and he recalled the desert origins of Israel's faith when he announced it. Unless the Jews left their homes and business and went out into the desert to hear the announcement, they probably would not hear it at all.

We have learned in recent years that John was not the only Jew of his time who returned to the desert to discern more clearly the present activity of God. In the same desert region, not far from the place where John preached and baptized, an entire community of Jews resided at Qumran. They withdrew from the world and its business and devoted themselves to an austere life in common and the study of the Law. They too expected the deliverance of Israel, and they felt that they could not prepare for it unless they returned to the desert. Only there, they believed, could they live as God intended them to live; it is evident from their writings that they regarded themselves as the one true Israel, the people of the covenant. The Judaism of the cities and villages, in their opinion, had betrayed its destiny.

Jesus Himself, the new Moses and the new Israel, first went to the desert before He began to announce the Gospel of the kingdom. The forty years of Israel's wanderings in the desert are echoed in the forty days of the sojourn of Jesus in the desert. He experienced the full harshness of the desert, for He fasted the entire forty days. The story of the desert sojourn does not tell us that, like Moses and Israel and Elijah, he there found God, for the early Church knew that Jesus did not have to seek God as other men did. The story resumes the theme of the desert as a place of testing, for it is in the desert that Jesus, like Israel, was tempted. Here He proves Himself the new and genuine Israel, for He is superior to the seductions of the tempter. He does not betray God for gain or honor or power, as Israel had done. When He emerges from the desert He has demonstrated His claim to fulfil the destiny of Israel. He emerges charged with that strength which in Israelite tradition is acquired from the struggle of man against the desert. A later New Testament writer draws comfort from this episode; for we have here a high priest who is not without feeling for our weakness, since He was tested in all ways like us without yielding.[1] We can approach Him with the assurance that He is acquainted with the weakness which makes it necessary for us to ask forgiveness.

Finally, we read that St. Paul did not immediately after his conversion at Damascus take up the apostolate among the Gentiles which Jesus had committed to him, nor did he take counsel with any man, not even with the apostles in Jerusalem; instead he retired for three years to Arabia.[2] Arabia here can scarcely mean anything except the desert; with the desert background which we have sketched above there can be no doubt that Paul felt the need of the desert experience before he could begin the mission. Paul had found God, or rather God had found him, in an entirely unique vocation; nevertheless, the full meaning of the vocation could not be penetrated unless Paul retired to the traditional source of spiritual strength, the place where man meets God. There

---

[1] Heb 4,15. [2] Gal 1,16-17.

he could determine whether he fully accepted the vocation and all that it implied, and there he could reflect upon what its execution demanded. We usually think of Paul as a man of the Hellenistic city which he knew so well, the cosmopolitan traveller who was at home in so many urban centers; we do not think of him as another Elijah or John the Baptist. But before Paul plunged into the crowded bustling cities he had steeled himself by three years of rugged desert life; he does not explain why he spent three years in the desert nor what he did there. To those who knew Israelite traditions no explanation was necessary, and to those who did not no explanation was possible. The New Testament contains a number of allusions to the desert experience and the desert testing of Israel, both from Paul himself and from others;[3] the desert history of Israel is a type of the Christian spiritual experience, from which Christians may learn the meaning of what happens to them.

Across the Nile from the city of Aswan in Egypt and a mile or two downstream is an impressive ruin which, unlike most of the ruins of Egypt, is not a

---

[3]   1 Cor 10,5; Heb 3,7-19; Act 3,17.

relic of the work of the Pharaohs. It was once the monastery of St. Simeon, and it is one of the larger remnants of the great movement into the desert of the fourth and fifth centuries of our era. Although the site is only a short distance from the city, the division between the irrigated land and the desert in Egypt is so sharp that a short walk takes one out of this world. The monastery lies in an entirely dead wilderness of sand and rock, and the silence is palpable. Here we are near the origins of monastic life, which left buildings like this in the Thebaid, and in the desert near Antioch and Aleppo in Syria, and at the desert ruin of Mar Saba in Palestine not far from Qumran. Abandoned now, these ruins attest the weariness of the world which was so general in the late years of the Roman Empire and drove many men into the desert to see if perchance they could find there what the world did not offer. Quite often, it seems, they were merely in flight from a world which had grown intolerable; one cannot compare such flights to the desert with the sojourn of Jesus and Paul. The sad history of many of these monasteries attests the barrenness of a life which was as barren as the desert life. Seeking God in the desert demands more than a geographical change.

On the first Sunday of Lent the Church reads to us the Gospel of Matthew 4,1-11, which tells of the temptation of Jesus in the desert. Traditionally the season of Lent has been called a return to the desert for the Christian. I have set forth the biblical background of this allusion in the hope that the spiritual experience of the desert may be better understood. For a spiritual experience of the desert does emerge from the passages which are cited; the elements of this experience have already been mentioned, and we have only to bring them together.

We are not, of course, speaking of the desert as a geographical phenomenon; we are venturing into the somewhat insecure field of typology, where it is eay to find glittering generalities and lose sight of what the Bible says. But if there is a genuine typology here at all, it seems to lie not in the geographical features of the desert, but in the spiritual atmosphere of the desert as the Bible reveals it. The spiritual atmosphere is not divorced from the geographical features. Man is not a pure form; his moods and his thinking and his decisions do not exist in a world of beautiful and objective abstractions unaffected by sense perceptions and emotional disturbances. They are deeply affected by what he eats and drinks and how well he likes it, by the weather, by the scenery; our response to such environmental factors may not be deliberate, but it is no less real. The spiritual atmosphere of the desert is man's response to its gaunt and hostile face. It makes man aware, as we have noticed, that the universe is not simply his friend; it makes him aware that evil is real and active. It reminds him that he is never far from death. Against its threat the ideals and ambitions of the world beyond the desert look insignificant; and he learns that the one basic good which he must preserve at all costs is life. When he flees the desert to the security of civilization where the naked menace of death is hidden, is he to think that he is returning to reality or fleeing from it? Which is reality, the desert or the world outside it? When the Church invites us to sojourn in the desert, she would have us face the reality of death and evil and stop pretending that it does not exist.

The desert, we have seen, reduces the complexity
of life to a few simple and ultimate issues; in fact,
it reduces these issues to one, which is whether one
wishes to live or to die. If one wishes to live, one
must take the necessary means. The desert does not
forgive frivolity. The Church would have us breathe
the spiritual atmosphere of the desert and enjoy the
clarity of vision which the desert demands. In this
atmosphere and with this vision we can see that our
life is resolved into a few ultimate issues, and that a
decision must be made. She would have us create
spiritual atmosphere by the traditional austerities of
Lent; through them we learn, as the desert dweller
knows, that very little is needed to sustain life. If
we can ever for a short period of time treat the world
as if it did not exist, we shall learn that it is for practical purposes nonexistent, a sham reality. Against
the threat of evil and death it is unable to protect us.

It is in the desert that Israel and her great men
found God, and it is in this spiritual atmosphere that
the Church would have us seek God. She would
lead us into the desert, as Hosea describes Yahweh
leading Israel into the desert, and there God can

speak to our heart. Like Israel, we are entirely devoted to the acquisition of things like wool and flax,
grain and wine and oil, silver and gold; if God is to
speak to us, either we must go into the desert to hear
Him or He will snatch us from the security of our
little world and drop us into a vast silence where
nothing but His voice can be heard. In an appall-
ing vision Jeremiah saw the garden land blasted into
desert by the fierce heat of God's anger;[1] if men will
not return to the desert to find God, He will make
their cities a desert where no sound drowns out His
voice.

The Church wishes Lent to be a period of testing,
as the desert experience was a testing. How, we
may ask, are we tested? Surely the little abstinences
by which we exhibit our penitential spirit cannot
be considered a serious test. Nor did the Church
ever consider the mere flight into the desert, even
the frightening austerities of the Lents of earlier centuries, as the true testing of Lent. The test of the
Christian is whether he can withdraw from his habit-
ual desires and interests sufficiently to meet God
on God's terms. The abstinences of Lent in modern

---

[1] Jer 4,26.

times are scarcely more than a ritual symbol of our readiness to follow God into the desert; but the symbol ought to symbolize something. The Gospel of the first Sunday of Lent places before us some fundamental issues on which the attitude of most of us is ambiguous: wealth, honor, and power. One need not desire much of these to desire them to excess; the world has suffered more from little Napoleons than it has suffered from big ones, and the greed of a million little men corrupts us far more than the occasional raids of a really great thief. The desert has no room for men of this stamp, and if we enter the spiritual atmosphere of the desert we are tested to see whether we are what we profess to be.

It appears, then, that the Bible and the Church tell us that we must go into the desert, the very embodiment of evil and death, in order to find life. And indeed they do. But is the paradox of this invitation any other than the paradox uttered by Jesus Himself, who tells us that he who wishes to save his life must lose it?

The Judge of All The Earth

The Judge of All The Earth

IT IS a curious accident of language that Hebrew has no single word which can be translated as "justice." Like other accidents of language, this defect in the Hebrew vocabulary reveals a deep difference between the mind of the Israelites who wrote the Old Testament and our own ways of thinking. We have inherited our ideas of law and justice from Greece and even more from Rome; these two ancient civilizations have given us the ideas and words. In our political thinking justice is the supreme virtue of civil society from which all other virtues flow; and a government which fails to render justice to its citizens is so corrupt that it ceases to be a legitimate government which can claim the allegiance of its citizens. Hebrew has several words for law, perhaps none of which correspond in meaning and use to our English word law; one of the most commonly used words we translate literally "judgment," the verdict of the judge. If we wish to translate "justice" into Hebrew, we shall do it best by combining two words. Where we think of justice, the Israelite thought of "righteous judgment." The phrase does not imply juridical positivism, as a modern reader could easily infer. It does imply the absence of an abstract idea of justice. Justice was produced by the verdict of the judge, who is the source and defender of justice. There is no "higher justice" above the law and the judge to which the Israelites would think of appealing. Nothing is just until it is judicially declared. For justice had no reality for the Israelites unless it was, as we would say, effectively realized; and only the declaration of the judge could give to justice concrete reality.

In spite of the intense activity of our courts, most of the citizens of our country have never had a personal encounter with the majesty of the law incarnated in the person of the judge on the bench. The novel, the theater, and the cinema have made us all familiar with the most awesome judicial action of English law; the judge puts on the black cap and pronounces the words which terminate the earthly life of a human person. This is total justice, and we can conceive of no greater judicial power. The judge is merely the officer of society; but when he pronounces the sentence of death, many feel that he assumes an attribute of God. It is not, I fear, for this reason that so many are convinced that neither society nor its officers have the right to pronounce this sentence. But this is our idea of the judge; behind the judge who imposes a fine for a traffic violation stands the hangman. Nothing keeps the judge from summoning the hangman for the traffic violation except abstract justice, embodied in written law.

When we join ourselves to the prayer of the priest with which the sacrifice of the Mass begins, we take a phrase from the Psalms and ask God to judge us. Most of us feel that this is an extremely bold approach; we hope that He will not take our prayer seriously. In our ways of thinking the good citizen is one who never has any occasion to encounter a judge; to invite the judge to pronounce a verdict is to invite the officer whose minister is the hangman. But this prayer was not written by a citizen of England or the United States, and it means something altogether different. Where the judge is the source

LIBRARY ST. MARY'S COLLEGE

and defender of justice, he is the saviour and the deliverer. To render judgment is to vindicate a claim. In the primitive thought and speech of early Israel a claim is righteous when it is mine; and the judge renders righteous judgment when he delivers a verdict in my favor. In the oldest conceptions of God judgment is an attribute of salvation.

This is evidently a rather primitive idea of justice, and we shall see that the growth of Israel in its faith and its knowledge demanded a growth likewise in its conception of justice. But in Psalm 7,7; 9,5; 42,1 and other prayers, the Israelite candidly asks God to judge him where it is clear that he is asking God to defend him. The judgment of God is the attribute by which he redeems Zion from the attacks of its enemies.[1] Because God is a God of judgment Israel can await in confidence the works of His grace and pity.[2] Because of the sins of Israel judgment is remote;[3] judgment here is evidently deliverance, for we would say that sins bring judgment near. The man who anounced the defeat and death of Absalom declared that God had "judged" David from his enemies.[4] Solomon's prayer at the dedication of the

---

[1] Isai 1,27.   [2] Isai 30,18.   [3] Isai 59,9.   [4] 2 Sam 18,31.

temple appeals to the judgment of God to forgive
the sins of His people — surely a paradoxical expression.[1] In this quality of judge God is frequently
called the defender of the poor, the orphan and the
widow.[2]

Where the judge is conceived as one who is on
your own side, he is evidently not on the side of
your enemies. To the enemies of Israel God is the
vindictive judge. He is the judge of the world and
of nations; in his appointed judgment he rises in
anger against the enemies of Israel.[3] The judgment
which he passes on the world in righteousness and
on peoples in equity is a condemnation.[4] When he
judges nations he shatters kings on the day of his
anger.[5]

Why is God the judge-defender-avenger of Israel
and the judge-adversary of the nations? Simply because he is united to Israel by a covenant of his own
election and establishment. Between God and Israel, in the unsophisticated thinking of early Israel,
a relationship arose like the relations of the members
of the family and clan. These groups preserved

---

[1] 1 Kg 8,49. [2] Deut 10,18; Ps 75,10;81,3;103,6;139,13; Job 36,6.
[3] Ps 7,7. [4] Ps 9,8;95,13. [5] Ps 109,6.

themselves from extinction by solidarity against all other groups; the individual demanded and received from the group the protection of his person and his claims, as he accepted the responsibility of defending the persons and claims of others. God is the "judge" of Israel because he is the kinsman and the avenger.

The prophetic revolution of the eighth and seventh centuries B.C. in Israel raised the question of this relationship. What happens if one of the parties is unfaithful to the obligations of the covenant? The relationship is like the relationships of family and clan, but it is also unlike them. Israel can release God from his promises by failing to fulfil its own. If it loses its fidelity, its only claim to the "judgments" of God, it must expect the judgment which he renders to the nations. By the time of Ezekiel, the early sixth century B.C., it was established in prophetic speech that the judgments of God upon Israel were not his saving acts but his punishments. In these as in his saving acts God exhibited the righteousness which is the essential quality of the judge. It is not righteous for him to treat virtue and sin equally. When this was perceived, Israel was educated in the concept of justice. Like all men, Israel also stands under judgment at all times.

It is not characteristic of Old Testament thought to conceive the judgment of God upon mankind in terms of a vast assizes to which all humanity is summoned, although the image is used in Joel[1] and Daniel.[2] The Old Testament regularly sees the judgments of God in the events of history or the catastrophes of nature. Judgment is not deferred to a far off eschatological event, but is executed here and now. The Israelite prophets reject any suggestion that the events of history and the catastrophes of nature are merely casual, needing no explanation other than the concurrence of various opposing forces. These vindicate the judgment of God on men and nations.

The idea of judgment passes from the Old Testament into the New Testament, and, like so many theological ideas, experiences a transformation. If one consults the concordance of the New Testament, it is at once evident that the words "judge" and "judgment" and compounds of these words occur

---

[1] Joel 4, 9-16.   [2] Dan 7, 9-12.

much less frequently in the Synoptic Gospels than they do in the Pauline and Johannine writings. The content of the Gospels bears out the statistics of the concordance; judgment is not a really dominant theme in the Synoptic Gospels. This does not imply that it is absent. Judgment is that which inevitably follows sin.[3] The judgment is usually mentioned without further details, and the interpreter wonders whether it refers to a judgment of this world or the next — in modern theological terms, whether the judgment is historical or eschatological. This question is of more importance than one might think; and we shall return to it later in this article.

Paul is much more conscious of the judgment than the authors of the Synoptic Gospels, so conscious indeed that it is troublesome for the interpreter who attempts to synthesize his thoughts. There is a past judgment, a sentence of condemnation which has fallen upon all men. This is the judgment passed upon all men in their ancestor,[4] who by his act brought all of humanity into a state of guilt. From his origin upon the earth man is under judgment. It

---

[3] Mt 5, 21-25; 12, 40-42; 23, 13,33; Mk 12,40;
Lk 10, 14; 11, 31-32; 12, 58.   [4] Rom 5, 16, 18.

is this thought of Paul which was the occasion of Augustine's famous and harsh phrase for unredeemed man, **massa damnata.** The saving act of Jesus Christ is an annulment of the judgment.[5] The judgment is a judgment of death; Jesus by his death restores life to the condemned.

But there is also a future judgment in Paul, and the future judgment is more prominent in his writings than the past judgment. This is the judgment which the sinner cannot escape.[6] It is a judgment accomplished on the day of wrath,[1] a day when God will judge the world,[2] the living and the dead.[3] One of his readers might have asked Paul whether a race condemned in its origin is capable of further judgment. But since neither his readers nor Paul himself placed the question, we must answer it ourselves, or find a reason why the question should not be asked. The answer here as so often in the theology of Paul lies in the versatility — one might say the mercurial quality — of Paul's thought. And the key here is perhaps that the judgment of all men in Adam is original with Paul, while the future judg-

---

[5] Rom 8, 1, 3.   [6] Rom 2, 1-3.
[1] Rom 3, 5.   [2] Rom 3, 6.   [3] 2 Tim 4, 1.

ment was an existing commonplace which Paul accepted. Here it is necessary to supply some information from extrabiblical sources.

The idea of judgment in the Old Testament sketched above experienced remarkable development in Jewish apocalyptic literature of the first century or two before the Christian era. In many of these writings the judgment of God on the nations was dramatized into a vast assize to which all men are summoned. Not infrequently this dramatic scene is painted in vivid and gruesome colors. The interest in apocalyptic literature (as the name of the literature indicates) lay in alleged revelations concerning the world catastrophe, the great act by which God overturns the world and vindicates His supremacy and His justice. This is the final victory of God over evil.

It is important to notice that the biblical belief in the final victory of God over evil is not of necessity linked with any particular dramatic or metaphorical expression. The last judgment scene which is depicted over so many cathedral doors and so many high altars has become in popular belief an article of faith scarcely less sacred than the Trinity of persons, and one accepts certain risks if one points out that an article of faith does not include purely artistic features. In the Synoptic Gospels the last judgment scene is reflected only in Matthew,[4] not paralleled in the other Gospels. Nor is it certainly reflected even there. The scene is not called a judgment, it does not resemble a judgment scene, nor are any legal terms employed. One may appear to be playing with words to dwell upon this, but legal terminology was available to the New Testament writers when they wished to use it, and they frequently did. If we call the scene in Matthew the last judgment, we are using a term which Matthew did not use.

With these reservations, one must still say that the apocalyptic judgment of Jewish belief is most probably what is implied in the judgment mentioned in the Synoptic Gospels and in the future judgment of Paul. Sound method demands that when we take this as an acceptance of the belief in a final "judgment" in the biblical sense, we are not compelled to a literal acceptance of the apocalyptic imagery in which this belief is sometimes expressed. Man is

---

[4] Mt 25, 31-36.

under a judgment from which he can escape, if he accepts the saving act of Jesus Christ; there awaits a judgment from which no deliverance can be expected. The terms of this judgment are man's response to his encounter with God in Jesus Christ; it is altogether fitting that the judgment of man's decision in this crisis should be committed to him who is the focus of the decision, the Lord Jesus Christ who comes to judge the living and the dead.

The judgment is a dominant theme in the Gospel of John; and it is presented in what appears at first sight to be a complex of paradoxes. Jesus came into the world not to judge the world but to save the world;[1] yet Jesus has come into the world for judgment.[2] The Father judges no one;[3] yet it must be the Father who seeks the glory of Jesus and who judges.[4] The Father judges no one because he has given all judgment to the Son,[5] and Jesus says that he judges justly[6] and truthfully.[7] Yet Jesus says he does not judge.[8]

The unity of thought which underlies these paradoxes is the entirely distinctive concept of the judg-

---

[1] Jn 3, 17; 12, 46.   [2] Jn 9, 39.   [3] Jn 5, 22.   [4] Jn 8, 50.
[5] Jn 5, 22, 27.   [6] Jn 5, 30.   [7] Jn 8, 16.   [8] Jn 8, 12; 12, 47.

ment presented by John. There is a judgment of the last day in John[9] and a resurrection of judgment which is contrasted with the resurrection of life.[10] But when one assembles the passages in which the judgment occurs in John, it is clear that the judgment is not past or future; it is present, it occurs now. The unbeliever is already judged.[11] The judge of the unbeliever on the last day is the word which Jesus has spoken.[12] The spirit proves that there is judgment by showing that the prince of the world is already judged.[13] The judgment of the world occurs now, when the decisive hour of the rejection of Jesus by his own people is near.[14]

What is this judgment which is eternally present, which is not the work of the Father but is committed to the Son? John has transformed the judgment from an act of God to an act of man; it is man who pronounces judgment upon himself. Jesus is judge in the sense that he is the object of decision; in this sense the Father judges no one but commits all judgment to the Son. In the same sense Jesus comes not to judge the world but to save the world; the decision

---

9 Jn 12, 48.   10 Jn 5, 29.   11 Jn 3, 18; 5, 24   12 Jn 12, 48.
13 Jn 16, 11.   14 Jn 12, 31.

is judgment or salvation to the man who makes it. In John the judgment is unbelief, refusal to accept Jesus as the Son. This judgment is pronounced when one encounters Jesus.

Effectively, then, John tells Christians that it is nonsense to await the judgment; the judgment is an accomplished fact, accomplished by the personal decision of each one. The "world," which in John's language means those who do not believe in Jesus, is judged by his very coming. Apocalyptic expectations can degenerate into an unreal dreamworld which has little reference to present reality; more than once in the history of Christianity they have been a refuge for those who felt defeated by the world. By recalling that the judgment is accomplished now by the personal decision of each man, John recalls Christians to a sense of their own responsibility and to the immediate effects of their decisions.

If these be the implications of the judgment as it is presented by John, they must have certain repercussions in the personal life of the individual Christian which are not always felt clearly. Christian humility is explained in such a way that the Christian learns to have a low esteem of his personal importance and value; and as a corrective of the pride and vanity which is natural to man the lessons are not to be dismissed. But humility, like all the virtues except love, becomes a distortion of the Christian ideal unless it is taken as part of a larger whole. The Christian who has become so humble that he believes his own personal decisions are important to no one, even to himself, is fleeing from Christian virtue, not pursuing it. What St. Paul meant when he said that the saints will judge the world[1] was clearer to him that it is to us. But it is not impossible that an element of the Johannine judgment crept into his language here, and that he meant that the lives of the saints will prove that the world which rejects Jesus Christ is wrong. Effectively the judgment of God in the present world is expressed in the lives of those who believe in him. And it is terribly important that those who believe in him should vindicate his judgment in what they say and do.

There is a judgment of God in history; and history is the actions of man in society. Just as history is a complex and protracted process and not a single ac-

---

[1] 1 Cor 6, 2.

tion, so the judgment of God in history is not a single event. The Bible is calmly assured that the history which is dominated by the saving acts and judgments of God is none the less written by the men whose decisions determine the events. The celebrated problem of the sovereignty of God and the freedom of man is not a genuine problem in the books of the Bible. One may say that this is due either to a more profound insight in the biblical writers or to their incapacity for the type of philosophical reflection which presents the problem. For one reason or the other, the Bible affirms each of these truths without losing its grasp on the other. And therefore John can present the judgment as both the action of God and the action of man. Surely one who knows that he shares in the formation of the judgment of God can scarcely think of his own personal decisions as unimportant. History is woven of these personal decisions, so closely interlocked between man and man and in the course of the personal life of each man that no one can set a limit to the consequences of his decisions. Each of us writes history each day, and when we write history we write God's judgment.

The personal decision which is judgment is never made by each man in the permanent and final form which makes further judgment impossible and unnecessary until each man is himself removed from history. The "now" of the judgment is not an instant; it is the "now" of the present life, of all the days and years in which we encounter Jesus Christ the incarnate Word. And indeed the word "encounter," so popular in modern theological writing, is not the perfect word to denote the unique experience of the personal meeting between God and man which occurs when the Word is made flesh and dwells among us. The reality of Jesus Christ is too immense to be apprehended in a single instant and in a single decision. Neither total acceptance of him nor total rejection of him is a decision easily and quickly made. In either case one learns anew each day of one's life what the reality is which one has accepted or rejected. And the magnitude of the decision, as well as its incalculable consequences, are not seen by us in their fullness. One decision leads infallibly to another, and the more one advances in the chain of decisions the more difficult it becomes to reverse the series. At what point does one really make a final and irreversible decision? The Church tells us that our judgment is not determined until we have passed from the land of the living. The Church as well as experience also tells us that men rarely abandon the decisions which have made them to be one thing rather than another. Each of these personal decisions is a factor forming the judgment which is not reversed.

In the thought of St. John, Jesus judges the world by his very coming and presence. I have paraphrased his thought by saying that Jesus is the judge by being the object of decision rather than its agent. It is a recurrent theme in St. John that the Jews who encountered Jesus did not recognize their judgment in him, and that their failure to recognize him is no excuse. The transparent reality of God in Christ can be concealed only by those who wish to conceal it. That transparent reality is the risen Jesus Christ living in his Church. St. John tells us that men judge themselves; and the entire New Testament, with one accord, tells Christians with more severity than usual that the judgment of other men does not belong to the Christian. The Christian can ask himself and not others whether the transparent reality of the risen Jesus living in His Church is dimmed and obscured to the world by himself; for each of us is the Church in his own time and place. He can ask himself whether in him the world sees the Church as essentially and primarily a community of love and not as something else. He can ask himself whether men will encounter Christ in the Church if they think, for reasons which are not entirely spurious, that the Church is a power society whose officers seem more interested in total control than in total dedication. He can ask himself whether men encounter Christ in a community where words like "due submission to properly constituted authority" are heard far more frequently than such words as "A new commandment I give you, that you love one another," and "Let him who would be first among you be the slave of others." He can ask himself whether the fullness of Christ has ever been revealed in the existent reality of the Church, and he will conclude that it has not because the members of the Church have not received the fullness of Christ

— because they did not choose to receive it. And he must admit that the reality of Christ can be most effectively concealed by those whose responsibility in the Church is the greatest.

It is not ours to judge any except ourselves; but we know that what dulls the encounter between the world and Christ in his Church is one thing here and now, another thing there and then. Can the Christian honestly take refuge from responsibility, which is his own judgment, because he thinks that leadership has failed him? Is he genuinely responsible if he shows a great readiness to do what is right only as long as everyone else has done it before him? Can he take real comfort in the thought that if what he is doing is, as he fears, wrong, at least he is doing wrong under clerical leadership? At one time in English history a layman, Thomas More, took a position in which he was supported by only one of the English bishops. We sometimes seek in the Church and her leadership a security which the Church does not promise: the security which is felt in blindly following directions which we know are not good, the assurance that we can safely let someone else do

our personal thinking and make our personal decisions. This is a flight from judgment. That more
men have not faced their own crisis as Thomas More
faced his is due simply to the fact that few of us are
aware of our responsibility as Thomas More was.
In him and those who like him made their own decision, and only in them, could one see Christ in His
Church in the England of his time. It would be a
mistake to think that this situation is unique.

One final aspect of the judgment as John conceives
it may further enlarge our understanding of judgment. John returns to the primitive biblical conception of judgment in this respect, that it is the
coming of Jesus as saviour that places man under
judgment. Jesus judges by his saving act and saves
by his judgment. Judgment becomes again deliverance in a more profound sense. When we combine
this with another aspect of the Johannine thought
in which judgment is transformed from an act of God
to an act of man, it appears that we have the saving
act also transformed from an act of God to an act of
man; and this is a heresy which the Church has re-
pudiated vigorously and often. Like all heresies,

this one is a distortion of a truth. John, like Paul, has no doubt that God alone saves and that man is incapable of saving himself. The act by which man judges and saves is the creation of God's saving and judging will within him. Man himself must make the decision; but he could not make it if God had not empowered him to make it. He is saved when he is judged, when he encounters Jesus Christ, the object of decision.

For the Christian the judgment is an object of hope rather than an object of fear. When we attribute judgment to God, we use a human term which can be misinterpreted if the analogy is pushed too hard. The judgment of God is not an act of law, for law is above the judge. God alone can pronounce a judgment which is a deliverance. The human judgment which we know cannot be exercised unless the judge lays aside love and mercy. The judgment of God is a judgment of love and mercy; were it anything else, it would not be the judgment of God.

The Growth of Expectation

MAY it not be that the development of eschatological expectation in the life of the Church is recapitulated, in some manner, in the spiritual development of every individual — that is, an initial burst of apocalyptic enthusiasm of first fervor, followed by a long pull of fidelity in the spirit of the Epistle to the Hebrews, maturing gradually into a Johannine awareness of the Trinity within us?[1]   Fr. John Bligh's three stages of the spiritual growth of the individual perversely reminded me of a witticism I once heard in Boston; and for the benefit of readers who are not acquainted with New England I should notice that the Boston ecclesiastical area long has been celebrated for wise sayings which play on biblical and liturgical Latin. This was long before the vernacular movement.   The saying described the three stages in the life of a bishop or an ecclesiastical superior in the opening words of terce, sext and none for Sunday according to the old Latin

---

[1]   THE WAY, Vol I (Oct 1961), p. 279.

psalter: the beginning of the exercise of authority, **Legem pone,** lay down the law; the middle phase, **Defecit spiritus,** the spirit grew weak; the final phase, **Mirabilia,** everything is wonderful. This summary of the ecclesiastical career is not entirely fanciful; and I think it is a kind of counterpart to the three phases described by Fr. Bligh. The critical point obviously lies in the middle phase. At this point one either settles down to "a long pull of fidelity," or one loses heart and begins the long decline into contentment with mediocrity.

When one looks at the apostolic Church, one is impressed by just those features which are missing or less prominent in the contemporary Church. The activity of the spirit took different and startling forms. There is only a sketchy structure of authority. There is an utter simplicity of doctrine and of practice. Yet when one looks at this Church closely, one sees that the Church could not retain permanently its apostolic form. When we consider what the apostolic Church did, we should also consider some of the things which it did not do. One should not think that only in the apostolic period did the Church realize her full potentiality, and that everything since the apostolic period represents a deterioration. The development of the post-apostolic Church represents neither a net gain nor net loss. Change had to come.

It may be over-simplification to say that the eschatological thrust of the apostolic Church delayed the development of form and structure; but it appears altogether probable that the two factors are related. If the parousia was imminent, then there was no need to think of a durable structure for the Church. Faith, repentance and baptism would create a community of love which would endure until Jesus returned. Why should any more than this be necessary? When Paul can spend some time reassuring the Thessalonians that those who have died before the parousia shall suffer no disadvantage compared to those whom he addresses, we can see in what direction the thought of the apostolic Church was running.[1] Such thinking would not lead the Church to plan for an indefinite future.

But the time did come when a decision had to be made, and the Church made it. It is impossible to

---

[1] I Thess 3, 13-18.

trace the steps by which this decision was made; but by the end of the first century the Church had prepared herself to face a future to which no definite end could be assigned. The mission of the Church was not to be realized briefly and quickly by a few brilliant strokes. The structure of the apostolic Church could not endure for a period of indefinite length; and some of the qualities of the apostolic Church had to yield for the sake of permanence and stability. The Church recognized that she possessed the resources of permanence and stability for an indefinite future. The spirit would operate in new ways adapted to the conditions of such a mission. The works of the spirit, suited to her mission, would endow the Church with an inner strength great enough for her to maintain her character against the erosion of time and the experiences of cultural change. Her expansive power would not be diminished, but would be combined with qualities of endurance through which she would not be distorted by rapid expansion. All this adds up in the practical order to a more rigid structure; and this is what the post-apostolic Church began to acquire.

There were risks in this development; and while it would be interesting to recite these risks, they need not be recited here. We in the modern Church know them well enough anyway. That risk which is pertinent to our reflections here is the risk of weakening hope by deferring it. The later Church undoubtedly does not have that type of strength which rises from a lively eschatological consciousness; and it should be noticed that I say "that type of strength." The growth of the Church in permanence and stability implies the risk of tacit acceptance of existing conditions as the permanent and terminal reality in which the Church and her members shall find their fulfilment. A parallel may be ventured between the Church in the world and Judaism in the world. For the survival of Judaism it may not have been necessary that Judaism should submerge its own native eschatologism; but the fact is that Judaism did reach a form so weak in its eschatological awareness that eschatology may be called simply unimportant in the ideas of recent Judaism. The Church has not abandoned her eschatological teaching; but the question of how meaningful this teaching is can be raised.

The Church is secularized to that degree to which she is eschatologically insensitive.

Together with this risk we can consider two other risks involved in hope deferred. The first of these is the risk of diminishing confidence in the Spirit as the agent of God's saving work. The works of the Spirit in the post-apostolic age are no less marvelous than those of the gifts of miracles and tongues, indeed they are more marvelous; but they do not excite the attention and admiration which were given to the phenomena of miracles and tongues. The more subtle workings of the Spirit can be easily mistaken for the works of something else than the Spirit. The post-apostolic Church can think of its ends as achieved by quite human methods adapted to the holy purposes of the Church. Secular means do at times appear to achieve the ends of the Church; what does not appear is the price which the Church pays for this type of success. The price can be, quite simply, her integrity; and this is, of course, a dreadful price to pay. When the Church becomes aware of this price, she may withdraw in horror but also in discouragement, thinking that what cannot be achieved through secular means cannot be achieved at all. She may not look to the Spirit for power.

Another risk involved in this attitude is the risk of engagement with the world. The Church is engaged with the world by her constitution and her mission. She is Christ living in the world, and she is the agent through which God transforms the world. But she cannot live in the world and proclaim the gospel to the world without close association with the world. She lives in constant danger that the transformation process will be reversed; and her history shows that the danger of secularization is never remote. What happens to the Church when she does not resist secularization need not occupy our attention here; but we can notice that she may resist the world by flight from the world, by refusing to be engaged with the world. Effectively this is to deny her mission to the world. The withdrawal may take many forms; the most recent form is that of the beleaguered fortress. In this way or in another, the Church ceases to be the transforming agent which she ought to be; she ceases to be the presence of Christ among men.

Can one say that the third stage of mature awareness of the Trinity within us is ever reached by the
Church in the world? No doubt there is an eschatological consummation which is not attained by the
Church in the world; but we have remarked that
the Church is an eschatological reality. If we dis-
tinguish these three stages with Fr. Bligh, then we
shall have to say that the Church attains the third
stage by achieving the second. When she recognizes
her true self and her true mission, then she is aware
of her identity with Christ and of the indwelling
spirit. She recognizes the Trinity of persons within
her by the dynamic of love; for love and love alone
is the active presence of God, Father, Son and Holy
Spirit in the world. She knows that men must encounter God in her; and she realizes the terrible responsibility she has of not interposing her fleshly
reality between them and God. She recognizes the
presence of God within her not by contemplating
her own grandeur, but by contemplating her own
poverty; and I do not mean poverty in the literal
sense of the word. I mean her poverty of spirit, her
lack of spirit, her insignificant works compared with

THE GROWTH OF EXPECTATION

the abundance of her resources, the many ways in which she fails to mirror the God who is love.

The Church never completes the task of defining herself to her members and to the world. She never attains a stage of development in which she is granted contemplation in repose. She must always work out the reality of the presence of Christ; that she has responded to challenges in the past does not assure her that she is meeting challenges in the present. The late Pope John XXIII brought the word **aggiornamento** into common use. He meant that the Church can never grow old. She is endowed with a permanent youth in the sense that she always remains flexible, possessed of reserves of strength, able to change and to adapt, not hobbled by custom and habit, not weary with prolonged toil, never without a future full of promise. She will never see the days of which she will say, I take no pleasure in them.

These are some reflections on the development of the Church suggested by the remarks of Fr. John Bligh; and it is time that we refer these reflections to the personal life of the individual Christian. Fr.

Bligh alluded to the phenomenon known as "first fervor," a phenomenon noted by all spiritual writers and experienced by everyone who seriously attempts to realize the Christian ideal. Generally those who write of first fervor write with a tone of warning against it. They believe that first fervor is like the seed in the parable of the sower, which takes root quickly and just as quickly withers in the sun or is choked by thorns or carried away by birds. First fervor is certainly an initial stage, it is open to excess of some kind almost by definition, and it must yield to something else. The locomotive, the automobile and the airplane are accelerated from a standing stop by opening the throttle full. The vehicle cannot be operated at full throttle for its entire course without burning out. But unless the throttle is opened wide when the movement begins, the vehicle will never move at all. And if one is to carry this figure of the early phase of the spiritual life any further, one cannot help remarking that the engine makes most noise when it is being accelerated. At the same time, every air traveller knows that the blast of the open throttle at take-off is a very com-

72

forting sound. And the noise of first fervor is also comforting.

The analogy should not be pressed too far, but it seems that the pentecostal fervor of the primitive Church must find its correspondence in the pentecostal fervor of the individual Christian if the Christian is to reach a more mature stage. The growth during first fervor, as far as it can be observed, seems to be incredibly rapid. The growth is manifested by external signs not as marvelous as the works of the Spirit in the apostolic Church, but which do cause wonder in those who behold them. The reign of God does seem to be just around the corner, and all one need do is to put one's soul in shape to receive it. Difficult deeds are accomplished with ease and even with joy. One is carried by a spiritual exaltation which is no less delightful for being more than slightly dangerous. For the beginner has not reached cruising speed, to carry on our metaphor, and he is really not very far off the ground. He is more aware of the distance he has traversed than he is of the distance which remains to be traversed; and because he has gone so far with relative ease, he does not know why he should not continue his course at the same pace and with the same ease.

He is generating power. Most Christians live on the convictions which they formed in their first fervor, as the Church lives on the spirit of the apostolic age. These convictions may indeed lack depth, and the Christian life in the initial phase is usually without plan and structure. In spite of the fact that this problem has been treated so many times in spiritual literature, it seems worthwhile to ask again what happens at that point where plan and structure should come, but do not; where something prevents the convictions generated during the first fervor from bearing fruit. There is a moment of decision, or rather a series of decisions, which issues either in the long pull of fidelity or the slow decline into mediocrity. The spirit fails — not the Holy Spirit, but the human spirit which does not respond to the Holy Spirit. The Christian remains spiritually immature; he falls into the "tepidity" of classical spiritual literature.

The analysis of this decline can be found in any of the classical works from Francis de Sales and Rod-

riguez to Thomas Merton. This writer has no inten-
tion of reading a lesson to these masters. But I suggest that they tend to conceive of this development
of the Christian as occurring in solitude, and it does
not; it occurs within the Church, within a community — religious or secular — and the decision of
the person is not entirely his own. It may in his
own mind meet the ideals of the community and
the possibilities which the community opens to him.
The reasons for his failure of spirit need not lie entirely within himself. That part of the Church in
which he lives may have done all it could to inhibit
the action of the spirit on its members. The individual may form his own decision in spite of his involvement in the community, but it is the exception-
al person who does this.

The critical decision, then, is made within the
community and not in isolation, and it is made under
the influence of the community. Consequently it
reflects the spirit of the community in which it is
made. The Church as a whole has accepted, of
course, the long hard pull of fidelity rather than the
slow decline into mediocrity; but this is not true of

the entire Church, and there have been times when the Church as a whole reflected tepidity rather than courage and perseverance in its mission. Some of the factors which influence the individual decision adversely deserve our attention, especially if we are in a position to do anything about these factors.

Poor direction receives full treatment in standard spiritual literature. In modern times incompetent direction probably does less harm than incompetent government in ecclesiastical offices and in religious communities, and we may take the two together. Failure to meet the spiritual crisis successfully may come from the fact that those who have the government or direction of the person refuse to allow him to make the decision. He may have been drilled to believe that he has no decisions of his own, that someone who stands in the place of God will make these decisions for him. He may have been taught to think that the Spirit will not move him except through the will of his superiors and directors. If he has learned his lessons well, he will await instructions on how to give form and structure to his Christian life. When the instructions never come, he will believe that he has done his own duty by not giving his life form and structure. He remains a perpetual adolescent in the spiritual life, never recognizing his mature powers and responsibilities. In this unnatural state it is scarcely possible for him to reach anything but mediocrity, for apparently this is what his directors wish him to achieve.

The power of personal decision may be inhibited by a rule of life which is too narrow and too antiquated for the situation in which the person must live. In the Church in general and in religious communities there is a veneration for tradition which at times approaches the pathological. Certainly tradition has its place, but we often have difficulty in defining its place. Excessive respect for the traditions of the elders caused problems long before the "new breed" appeared in seminaries and religious houses. Kindness forbids the citation of concrete examples. But all of us are acquainted with rules and customs which are so far out of touch with the contemporary scene as to be ridiculous, did they not sometimes have unfortunate effects in the lives of individual persons. One example which is fairly common and can be cited without offending anyone in particular is the refusal of religious communities to adjust their **horarium** to the customary hours of the world in which they are engaged. The **horarium** of most communities is based on the working day of the medieval European peasant. When this schedule is introduced into a large modern city, it usually means that the religious are awake when everyone else is asleep and asleep when everyone else is awake. Effectively it means that the religious may habitually deprive themselves of necessary sleep. Superiors who notice an unusual number of coronary occlusions among men in their fifties could give some attention to certain features of their customary life. Martyrdom for the sake of a traditional hour of rising does seem to be an unnecessary spilling of Christian blood, which ought to be saved for more worthy causes like righteousness and bearing witness to the name of Jesus.

The example may seem trivial, but the principle at stake is of utmost importance. Religious communities and seminaries should have noticed, if they have not yet done so, a larger number of young men who leave at the point of maturity than formerly. These communities have never had any trouble rationalizing defections; the very word defection illustrates rationalization at work. When these defectors say that they wish to do the work of God, but cannot do it in a narrowly rigid and antiquated routine, the communities put this down as a mask of discontent and an excuse for personal failure. Honesty demands that the question be examined from all sides, not merely from the side of the community. In the terms used in this article, these candidates see no future in the priesthood or the religious life other than the slow decline into mediocrity, and they refuse this. They seek elsewhere the life in which they can undertake the long pull of fidelity. They no longer accept the view that observance of the rule is a full time job worthy of the energy of a grown man.

Growth is a form of change, and the personal decision by which one accepts the life of fidelity is a high point of growth. We do not know how many people refuse the decision because they have been trained to resist change. Since the opening of the

second Vatican Council we have re-discovered the
inner resources of the Church which enable it to
adapt its form and structure to meet new demands,
and we have all marvelled at the manifest power of
the Spirit. We have also rediscovered the tremendous immobility of much of the membership of the
Church, which dislikes change in any area: liturgical
practice, biblical studies, the relation of the Bible
to tradition, the idea of the Church, the structure
of the Church, the attitude of the Church towards
the world, in particular towards Protestants and
Jews — every matter which has come up for discussion in the Council. In this school of thought there
is never any reason for doing something which is
not already being done, or for doing anything in a
way different from the way in which it has always
been done. The Christian who has been trained in
this school thinks of his personal life as he thinks
of the life of the Church, and it is difficult to put his
ideas in form. We may attempt to do so by saying
that his ideal is not to live his own life, but to re-
enact the life of others. For all that he must do he
seeks precedent, and when he does not find it he is

sure that it should not be done.

First fervor, we have remarked, generates power; and the power often rots because it is not exercised. At the point of mature decision the person may be denied legitimate outlets for the power which he feels within him. Here perhaps more than any other place the government of the Church sins against the spirit and against the members of the Church. This is not new in the Church. One need not be widely read in the lives of the saints and the history of the Church to know that every creative and imaginative step has been taken against opposition which at times seemed insuperable.

I seem to have proposed with more rhetoric than necessary the obstacles to the decision to settle down into the long pull of fidelity. One should not forget that there is a power greater than these obstacles, and that is the power of the Spirit. The pentecostal Spirit of the first fervor matures into the spirit of courage and patience by which one finds the fulfilment of the Christian life in spite of the factors which interfere with fulfilment. In speaking of the Church we outlined what seems to be the process of development, and we spoke of it as the finding of form and structure suited to the mission of the Church. We mentioned the risks involved in this transformation, and these risks can be transferred to the life of the individual Christian. He too may lose confidence in the Spirit; he may become secularized by accepting the condition of the Church and himself in the world as terminal, or he may flee engagement with the world in eschatological terror. The form and structure by which he is enabled to overcome these risks must be, like the form and structure of the Church, a form imposed by the Spirit and not by secular ends and means, even when secular ends and means are accepted by the Church in which he lives. He must recognize that the mission of the Church is his mission: to be the living presence of Christ in the world and the agent by which God transforms the world. In him men will encounter the God who is love. This mission cannot be frustrated even by members of the Church.

Like the Church as a whole, the Christian never finishes the task of defining himself as a Christian. The long pull of fidelity does not mean that he settles into a rut. He may bewail his lack of opportunities while at the same time he does not see the opportunities which the Spirit opens for him. Like the Church as a whole, he passes into the third stage of awareness of the Trinity by meeting the demands of the second stage. When he is moved by the dynamic of love, the Father, Son and holy Spirit come to him and dwell with him. God has in him created a new presence of himself in the world. And in this creation the eschatological reality has received a new dimension. The individual Christian as well as his fellow members of the Church must never forget that this dimension can be achieved only in this person. If it is not achieved in him, it will not be achieved at all.

An Exegete at The Manger

WITH the arrival of the Advent season and the Nativity-Epiphany cycle the interpreter of the Bible is tempted to crawl into his cave and remain there until some safe date like Septuagesima Sunday. The almost palpable dislike with which he is sometimes regarded is peculiarly acute at that season of the year. Too many people are convinced that exegesis is determined to destroy the historical reality of the events which are commemorated in the Nativity-Epiphany cycle. We have been asked by friends — half-seriously, I hope, but half — whether we can really take part sincerely in the celebration of these feasts. When the interpreter answers that he can, he is suspected of being a hypocrite.

Yet if the exegete flees, he is convinced that he is fleeing from an unjust attack. His studies of the infancy narratives of the Gospels have made the feasts of this cycle more meaningful rather than less.

It is difficult to explain how this happens, but I believe I ought to try. If exegesis did not make the details of the Christ event more meaningful, it would have little right to claim attention in the Church. If interpreters cannot communicate their own sentiments to their fellow Catholics, they must suffer from unusually serious impediments in thought or speech or both.

Many people believe that modern interpreters deny or doubt the historical reality of the annunciation, the visitation, the song of the angels, the visit of the Magi, the killing of the Holy Innocents and the sojourn in Egypt. It is probable, some think, that interpreters also doubt the Virgin Birth and the Divinity of the Word, but do not yet dare to say this in public. The interpreter becomes the butt of jokes when the crib is set up in the Church or in the monastery; his permission to erect it is jocosely asked, or he receives apologies for the offense that the crib must give his scholarly instincts. The interpreter goes along with these witticisms, because no one survives very long in his business without a sense of humor. But he does not care to have people think that his area of learning is out of touch with Christian belief and Christian piety.

Any interpreter knows that the interpretation of the infancy narratives is a piece of unfinished business. We do not yet have a satisfactory exegetical statement about the passages mentioned in the preceding paragraph; and it is just possible that the faithful ought to let interpreters finish the business which only interpreters can finish. It should no longer be necessary to argue — if it ever was necessary — that the details of the infancy are not historical in the same sense in which the crucifixion of Jesus is historical. Our problem is to define the sense in which these narratives are historical. Possibly a more solidly founded solution would be open to criticism, but criticism could await the presentation of the solution.

A second and fairly important point is this: the historical reality of the birth of Jesus is not in question. It will be conceded, I trust, that the birth of Jesus is the basic historical reality on which other things repose. The significance of this event does not depend on the details of the narratives in which it is related. These details have their place, as I intend to point out; but it is poor theology to place the historical reality of the Magi on the same plane as the nativity of Jesus. No exegetical discussion with which I am acquainted has touched those truths which are properly called dogmatic; and it is quite without foundation to say that this is the direction in which exegetical thought is moving. As one whose professional business it is to maintain some familiarity with exegetical thought, permit me to say that it is not moving in this direction.

Within these general cautions, let us view the problems from another angle which may be new to many. The galleries of Europe are full of Nativity scenes painted by Christian artists; many of the finest of these scenes are used on our Christmas greeting cards. It is pedantic, no doubt, to point out that none of these scenes has any resemblance to the historical reality which they represent. The landscape is never Palestinian; it is usually Tuscan, because so many fine artists lived and worked in Florence. The buildings are likewise unmistakably Italian Renaissance. More than that, the figures in the paintings either wear fifteenth or sixteenth century costume or a costume never worn by anyone; and their features are the features of the people whom the artists knew. The ox and the ass at the crib come from Isaiah 1:3, not from the Gospels. Consciously or not, the artists have shown that the Nativity is an enduring event contemporary to all times by transferring it to their own country and time. They have thus expressed a profound theological truth; but to express it they have had to renounce any attempt at a historical representation. Nothing is lost here, for none of them was capable of a historical representation; and I think most of them knew it.

This type of artistic treatment is regarded by no one as a distortion of the historical reality. Since the Magi cannot be painted in their proper costume, we could protest that they should appear simply as faces and not as figures. But the artist is allowed his liberties; and sometimes the more liberties he takes, the better we like him. We have learned that painting is more than photography, and that it conveys more of the meaning of that which it represents than photography can. Poetry too can open insights which sober and precise prose and statistics do not. The artist is helpless without the symbolism of art; if he is limited to that which can be verified historically, he cannot paint that which he most wants to paint: his own personal insight into the reality which he portrays. The face of Botticelli's Venus appears in some other paintings as the face of the Madonna. If one wished to be captious about this, one could make some incisive remarks about fidelity to the historical realities. For many people, the image of the Madonna is drawn from Botticelli.

There is a symbolism of literature as well as a symbolism of painting and sculpture. Imaginative literary symbolism is everywhere accepted as a part of conventional language; and there is no good reason why symbolism should not have its place in the Bible too. But the suggestion that this art form is found in the Bible is often greeted with suspicion as a covert attack upon the historical reality of the events of salvation history. Somewhere in this suspicion there lurks an affirmation that literary symbolism, legitimate in other writings, is not a legitimate form of expression in the Bible. This affirmation must be justified before any arguments can be founded upon it; and there is, of course, no justification for it. Literary symbolism does appear in biblical narratives; whether it is present or not in any particular passage is to be determined by an examination of the text, the context and the book and not by general judgment formed without references to the particular question.

Why should we think that there is literary symbolism in the infancy narratives? The interpreter holds that it is a sound principle to look for some symbolism when there are reasons for wondering whether the narrative before him is meant to be a simple recital of "facts." There are reasons for asking this about the infancy narratives. On the assumption that the infancy narratives are a simple recital of fact, a certain number of serious historical problems arise which it is the interpreter's task to solve. It is impossible to deal with these problems in this limited space, but no one should talk glibly about the historical character of the infancy narratives unless he has at least recognized that these problems exist.

LIBRARY ST. MARY'S COLLEGE

We have to explain how it is that Matthew and Luke are not only independent of each other, but why they cannot be harmonized. Matthew knows nothing of a previous residence in Nazareth, and Luke knows nothing of a killing of the Innocents and a flight into Egypt. Matthew knows nothing of a census, and there are good reasons why he should not; the only census of which we have knowledge was taken in Syria at a date which can in no hypothesis be adjusted to the date of the birth of Jesus, but which is too close to the probable date to allow us to suppose that another census was taken at the date which the narrative of Luke would demand. Josephus does not mention the killing of the Innocents; he was not the world's most careful historian, but he was deeply hostile to Herod, and it is absurd to suppose that he omitted the incident because of its Christian implications. Josephus has amply proved his ability to rewrite history in such a way that it serves his own purposes.

We have to explain the sources of Matthew and Luke; and while we are explaining this, we may deal with the question of why Mark's narrative begins with the baptism of Jesus. The picture of Luke sitting at the knees of Mary with his notebook in his hand is dear to devout tradition, but it has not a shred of foundation in historical evidence; it is a sheer assumption, no less sheer because it is devout. And if Luke sat at the knees of Mary for his information, Matthew must have been talking to someone else. There are other problems besides these; and one who asserts the pure historical character of the infancy narratives must deal with them. To dismiss them as irrelevant or to annihilate them by re-writing history is not candid.

The assumption that there is literary symbolism in the infancy narratives solves these problems; but a hypothesis is not proved because it answers questions. I should add that it is not disproved because it answers questions either; but at the moment I am not trying to prove any hypothesis. The question here is simply whether there is room for a hypothesis. As long as the historical problems mentioned above remain unsolved, there is clearly room; and we may look for literary symbolism in the infancy narratives. But we cannot look for literary symbolism in general. What we mean by literary symbolism here is the use of imaginative material to present a truth other than historical in narrative form. In the Gospels this truth is expected to be theological.

Let us return for a moment to the symbolism of the plastic arts, not because this symbolism is of the same order as literary symbolism, but because it is accepted without question. We will allow Botticelli, Angelico and their associates to paint the Nativity in a way which is almost totally unhistorical. We do not therefore say that the painting is untruthful. The birth of a male infant is in itself, of course, an exciting event; it is a crisis in the lives of the parents and in the life of the infant. The beginning of a new human life is an event of such moment that art and language are helpless in its presence; they are afraid of falling into sentimentalism and missing the deep reality of the event. Yet this exciting event is routine; it happens every day, every hour, every minute. That one can discern the whole wonder of creation in a single birth becomes obscure because of the prodigality with which life is dispensed. How shall the painter represent a scene at once so common and so thrilling?

AN EXEGETE AT THE MANGER

If a single typical birth scene is more than the talent and industry of a great artist can easily represent, surely that unique birth which was the Incarnation is even more difficult; but artists have been less hesitant here. The greatest Nativity scenes, in the opinion of this untrained observer, are those which have caught something of the miracle of birth; and these are few. But the artist was encouraged because the literary sources give him ample material for his artistic symbolism. They give him angels, shepherds, and wise men from the East. It is then up to him to surround his central figures with an unearthly luminosity which suggests that heaven and earth meet here, and to put on their countenances the expression of humble wonder which reveals the presence of majesty recognized. This birth scene is the encounter of man with God, the inbreak of God into history; this the artist knows he must portray, and no symbolism which portrays it is inept or illegitimate. In even the most rigid interpretation of the Gospels there is nothing to suggest that handsome, winged young men in white robes hovered over the infant and his mother; but I have never found them

offensive to my critical sense, because I know that
a celestial reality is extremely hard to paint.

The wonders which accompanied the birth in the
narratives of Matthew and Luke have left absolutely
no trace in the subsequent narratives of the Gospels.
Everything suggests that Jesus in His birth, as in His
life and death, shared fully the common portion of
man. The wonder of the Incarnation was perceived
in the Gospels by faith, and not by sensible appre-
hension. But the writer, like the painter, needs the
realities of the sensible world as symbols of the
realities of the spiritual world. Both Matthew and
Luke are clear that Jesus is not the natural son of
Joseph. Jesus is the Son of God, and they did not
think it enough to say this simply. I can hardly
quarrel with their effort to say it more emphatically.
On the assumption — which, as we have seen, can
be easily made — that they had little or no positive
information about the events of the birth of Jesus,
they had ample reason for filling this historical vac-
uum with a statement of the fundamental reality of
the Incarnation. That they chose a narrative form
instead of a philosophical form for the statement is

altogether in keeping with their known literary habits; neither Gospel contains a single philosophical statement.

It is evident from the Gospels that Jesus was extremely reserved about the kingship of the Messiah, and this reserve needs no explanation. It is somewhat surprising that most of the allusions to the messianic kingship are found in the infancy narratives. The paradox of kingship in infancy and poverty is evident, and it has furnished material for many sermons. The kingship of Jesus was always a paradox when it was seen in contrast to his human condition. Matthew and Luke are not so much concerned with affirming his kingship as with defining the type of kingship which the Messiah possessed. His kingship was not a rule of pomp and power; it was a kingship proper to him who called himself meek and humble of heart, and told his apostles that they should be the lackeys and slaves in the Church which he founded. No better opportunity to set forth this unique kingship could be found than the period in the life of Jesus when he showed the image of kingship least. The only explicit profession of kingship in the Gospels outside of the infancy narratives is found in the Gospel of John, where Jesus professes kingship when he stands as a prisoner about to be condemned to death.

A theme which runs through the Gospel of Matthew is that Jesus Messiah found faith among the Gentiles which he did not find among his own people. This haunting tragedy of the history of Israel always lies near the surface. It is explicit in Matthew's story of the Magi, unidentified men from a foreign country who come to Israel to seek that which Israel had in its midst without knowing it. The hatred of the Messiah which Herod shows is a prefiguring of the hatred of the Jewish leaders who bring Jesus to his cross. But Jesus is the Messiah of the world and not merely of the Jews; and the Gentiles who seek him will find him — indeed, God will lead them if they can find no human guidance. Efforts to frustrate the messianic mission cannot succeed; they may produce a blood slaughter — the Innocents die as Jesus died — but the saving act of God is not arrested by these plots.

A theme constant in Luke is also explicit in his

infancy narratives. Luke takes particular delight in presenting Jesus as the Messiah of the poor and the lowly, who is himself poor and lowly. This Messiah shows in the scene of his birth the traits which mark his mission. By a remarkable concatenation of circumstances the Messiah of the poor and lowly has no home in which he can be born. The first to bear witness to his messiahship are the poor and lowly, shepherds whose employment makes them temporarily homeless as he is homeless. The heavenly messengers are not sent to the great and the rich, but to those to whom Jesus will proclaim the Gospel. The Nativity scene of Luke is a narrative commentary on the words in which Jesus thanks the Father that he has hidden his saving plans from the wise and revealed them to the little ones.

These are some of the things on which the interpreter reflects as he reads the biblical narratives and as he is swept into the wealth of symbolism and imagery in the Nativity-Epiphany liturgical cycle. He does not know why others cannot share his reflections; for they differ very little from the traditional Christian reflections in this liturgical cycle. More than others he is sensible of the text just quoted, that the Father has hidden these things from the wise and revealed them to little ones. His wisdom is a demonic quality which at times can frighten him. But ignorance can be demonic too. The interpreter is awed not only by the majestic literary presentation of the Nativity event, but also by the unerring insight with which the Church has always discerned the reality and significance of the event. With or without discussions of the historical quality of the narrative, the Church has proclaimed the event of the Nativity as the Gospel proclaimed it; it is the advent of the Son of God, the King Messiah of the poor and lowly who demands a faith corresponding to the greatness of God's love revealed in the Incarnation.

The Scriptural Approach to Vocations

THE best way to ascertain the scriptural approach to vocations, although it is not the most sprightly way, is to see who are called in Scripture and what common elements we can find in these vocations. Vocations in the Bible begin with Abraham and end with the vocation of the Christian in the New Testament. Those called are kings, prophets, apostles and others with a peculiar mission or office, such as the judges of Israel, e.g., Gideon (Jgs 6:12-23), Abraham (Gn 12:1-3), Moses (Ex 3:1-4:17), and John the Baptist (Lk 1:13-17). The people of Israel as a whole is the object of vocation (Ex 19:3-5), and this concept is transformed in the New Testament to the vocation of the individual Christian (Rm 8:29-30; Gal 1:6-15; 1 Cor 1:26-30 and elsewhere).

For what are they called? Sometimes the purpose of the vocation is not specified; e.g., Abraham (Gn 12:1-3). More frequently it is. Moses and Gideon were called to deliver Israel. Saul and David were called to be kings of Israel (Ps 89:20-38; 1 Sam 9:15-16). The prophets were called to deliver the word of God to Israel (Is 6; Je 1:4-10), and the mission of the apostles is gradually unfolded in the course of the Gospels. Israel was called to be the people of the Lord, a kingdom of priests and a holy nation (Ex 19:5-6), transferred in the New Testament to the Christian (1 Pt 2:9).

How is the vocation manifested to the one called? In the Bible it is usually manifested through a direct address of God to the one called (Abraham; Moses; Gideon; Samuel; Isaiah; Jeremiah; Ezekiel; Amos; John the Baptist) or a direct invitation of Jesus Christ (the apostles) and sometimes through a prophet (Saul; David). Sometimes the vocation is an imperative rather than an invitation (Moses; Amos; Jeremiah); the unique vocation of St. Paul was a violent imperative. Without going into the questions of exegesis and literary form into which this consideration would take us, it is sufficient to note that a biblical vocation to a mission or office in which the work of God is accomplished is not conceived as genuine unless it is made clear in some way that God wishes the person to undertake the work. This is true also of the vocation of Isaiah, which is a response to a general invitation.

Frequently the one called is also called elect. Israel is the chosen one of the Lord (Is 41:8), as is the Servant of the Lord (Is 42:1; 49:7). David is the chosen one of the Lord (Ps 89:20). The choice sometimes included predestination from birth or before birth, as of the Servant of the Lord (Is 49:1), Jeremiah (1:5), John the Baptist (Lk 1:12ff), and St. Paul (Gal 1:15). The vocations of the apostles recorded in the Gospels were direct invitations of Jesus to individuals whom He selected and not general invitations (Mt 4:18ff; 9:9 and parallels). John wrote, "You have not chosen me, I have chosen you and appointed you" (Jn 15:15). Paul was a chosen vessel (AA 9:15): and when it became necessary to defend his apostolic commission he described himself as commissioned by God, not by men (2 Cor 2:15; Gal 1:1, 15).

It may be surprising to learn that biblical vocations exhibit a number of common elements which can be

traced through Old and New Testament and can ultimately be reduced to a few; and perhaps it is even
more surprising to learn that the common element
which appears most frequently is the assurance of
divine protection and assistance which guarantees
the success of the mission or the office. This appears in the earliest vocations of the Bible and the
latest. The Lord blesses Abraham and those who
bless him (Gn 12:2-3). The Lord brought Israel out
of Egypt·to make Israel His people (Ex 19:3). Gideon
is greeted with the assurance that the Lord is with
him and in his strength he shall save Israel (Jgs 6:12,
14). The hand of the Lord holds David firm, and the
arm of the Lord strengthens him, and his enemies
shall be defeated (Ps 89:22-24). Ezekiel will be made
as hard-faced and stubborn as the house of Israel,
who will not listen to his words (Ezk 3:7-9). The
Lord upholds His Servant (J42:1), helps him and
makes his face hard as flint (50:7). This assurance
of protection and assistance becomes doubly emphatic when the object of vocation pleads that he
is unequal to the task. Moses feared the unbelief
of Israel and was reassured by the power to work

wonders which was granted him (Ex 4:1ff), and when he urged his slowness in speech the Lord promised His help in speaking (Ex 4:10ff). Jeremiah felt unable to speak, and the Lord touched his mouth and put His words in the mouth of Jeremiah (Je 1:6-9). Against the resistance of Israel, the Lord made Jeremiah as strong as a fortified city, an iron pillar, and a bronze wall and assured him that his adversaries would never overcome him (Je 1:18-19). This assurance often is confirmed by the promise of the peculiar gifts which are necessary to meet the demands of the mission or office. The Lord puts His spirit upon His servant (Is 42:1), makes his mouth like a sharp sword (Is 49:2), and gives him a tongue for teaching (Is 50:4). Jesus gives His apostles power to cure the ill, to raise the dead and to expel demons (Mt 10:1-8; Mk 3:15; Lk 9:1-2). John the Baptist is filled with the holy spirit from his birth and will go in the spirit and power of Elijah (Lk 1:15, 17). St. Paul is confident not because he is self-sufficient, but because God has made him sufficient for his task (2 Cor 3:4-6); the power with which he is endowed comes from God and not from himself (2 Cor 4:7).

St. Paul tells us that it is one and the same spirit which endows the various offices in the Church with the gifts necessary to fulfill the office — apostles, prophets, teachers, wonder--workers, healers, administrators (1 Cor 12:4-11, 28-30). Each of these has his place and appointment in the Church from God (Eph 4:11) and together they make up its perfection.

This assurance is again emphatic when it is given against persecution which is often promised to those who have a vocation. We have noticed that Jeremiah and Ezekiel were assured of strength and perseverance against resistance and unbelief. The Servant of the Lord will be delivered to those who strike him and insult him, but because of God's help he will not give way (Is 50:5-8). Indeed it is through his death that the Servant will achieve his supreme victory (Is 53:1-12). Jesus assured His apostles that they should be persecuted. They must persevere; when they are expelled from one town they are to go to another. He promises them that the Spirit will give them the words they need (Mt 10:19-20; Mk 13:11; Lk 21:14-15). But they must fear nothing, even death itself, for they are in the hands of the

Father and even death will not defeat their mission (Mt 10:16-33). St. Paul also was assured of persecution; but he was the chosen vessel through whom the Gospel was to be carried to the nations and he would succeed (AA 9:15-16; 26:17-19). Here again it is not within the scope of this paper to enter into exegesis in details; but it is clear from these texts that it is a solid biblical belief that God does not call a man to a mission or office without granting him the necessary gifts, whether external or even gifts which are interior and personal, to carry out the mission. God does not guarantee the one called freedom from opposition, from pain and even from death; He does guarantee that He makes it possible to fulfill the vocation against any opposition.

A vocation often includes an express renunciation. Abraham must leave his home, his country and his relatives (Gn 12:2) for a mission as yet not specified. In the New Testament the element of renunciation becomes entirely explicit in the Gospels, at first in action and then in the demands which Jesus makes of those called. Those whom he first called to follow Him simply abandoned their homes, their work,

111

their families (Mt 4:18-22; Mk1:18-20; Lk 5:11; Mt 9:9; Mk 2:14; Lk 5:27-28). Jesus warns His apostles that the vocation will divide families (Mt 10:21, 35-37) and that they will be universally hated (Mt 10:22). St. Luke introduces three typical cases of those who could not accept the vocation because of family ties, and the words of Jesus are unbending: "The Son of Man has no place to lay His head;" "Let the dead bury their dead;" "No one who puts his hand to the plough and looks back is fit for the kingdom of God" (Lk 9:57-62). The one who follows Jesus must show a love of Jesus greater than his love of his family, and take up his cross to follow Jesus, with all that is implied in the word cross (Mt 10:37-38; Lk 14:26-27).

Jesus insisted particularly upon the renunciation of wealth. His instructions to His apostles forbade them not only to take money on their journey, but even to take what seem to be necessary supplies and equipment (Mt 10:9-10; Lk 10:4). We are all familiar in the context of vocations with the story of the rich young man from which the three evangelical counsels are deduced (Mt 19:16-24; Lk 18:18-23; Mk 10:17-22). With all due respects to the second and third of these counsels, they are implied in two words, while the first is explicit and given at some length: "If you want to be perfect, go and sell your property and get heavenly riches." It was this explicit recommendation which discouraged the man from pursuing the vocation any further. Jesus then went on to point out that this attitude not only prevented the man from becoming perfect, which he desired, and from following Jesus, which he also desired, but even from entering the kingdom of God; His disciples were appalled by this statement. We can generalize from these passages that a biblical vocation demands a total commitment with no reservations, even reservations which would be included in any conception of a normal life. The vocation demands that the one called accept a mode of life which is not normal, which has no parallel interests or activity, however innocent they may be, and no other demands on one's devotion.

The vocation is not without its rewards, but it must be said that these are neither tangible nor emphasized. When Peter, alarmed by the distressing words of Jesus about the impossibility of entry into the kingdom of heaven for the rich, said, "Look, we have left everything and followed you; now what are we to have?" Jesus answered that those who had made the renunciation to follow Him would sit on thrones judging the twelve tribes of Israel. Furthermore, they would receive a hundredfold of the worldly goods which they abandoned and would secure eternal life (Mt 19:27-29). Again we cannot descend to particular exegetical questions; I am sure you are aware that the history of the interpretation of this passage is not without interest. But again we can summarize that Jesus, when asked directly, affirmed that he did not demand a total commitment while offering nothing in return. He who made it would gain, not lose. That he would gain is something he must accept by faith.

A vocation brought the one called into a distinctive relation of intimacy with God. St. John says, "You are no longer slaves but friends" (Jn 15:15). He is associated with what is most distinctly the work of God. Among the many allusions in the

Pauline writings to the office of the apostle we find that the apostles are servants and stewards of the mysteries of God (1 Cor 4:1); they are the fragrance of God, vital and life-giving, uttering the message of Christ in union with Him (2 Cor 2:15-17); they are ambassadors of Christ (2 Cor 5:20) and God's fellow-workers (2 Cor 6:1).

Let me recapitulate the elements of the biblical concept of vocation. We see that a vocation is directed to a particular task, mission or office; that it is made known through a divine revelation; that it includes assurance of divine protection and assistance, of the means necessary to execute the mission, and of success; that it includes the possibility, indeed the likelihood of persecution; that it is a total commitment demanding renunciation; that it brings one near God; and that it is rewarding.

I think the idea of the Christian life as a vocation is important, although it would take too much space to bring out all its facets. In the New Testament view one has not a vocation to the Church and then to an office or mission in the Church, but one has a vocation to some position in the Church. The

Christian vocation is fulfilled by some in the lay state, by others in the clerical state. St. Paul mentions the almsgiver in the same series with the apostle, prophet, and doctor. To understand this is to understand the unity of the Church in one body, which is the point of the context where this occurs; and it surely ought to promote vocations if our young people are aware that the gulf is not as great as they think between what we call "vocational" states and the lay or secular state. For St. Paul all members of the Church are called.

The vocation through a direct or prophetic communication of God obviously needs to be reinterpreted in our times. Our seminaries and novitiates would be empty — or at least much more sparsely populated — if candidates came only after an experience like that of Samuel or Isaiah. Nor would they await such a communication. The Church is the living Christ which carries on His work and the Church extends the invitation which Jesus extended to His apostles. But she does not use the method of selection which He employed; instead she issues a general invitation to all to ask themselves whether they have the desire and the qualification to fulfill their Christian vocation in the clerical or religious state. For the candidate the genuinity of the vocation is ultimately validated by the acceptance of the Church through the diocese or the religious community. It is scarcely necessary, I trust, to remind ecclesiastical and religious superiors of whose function they fulfill when they accept candidates to admission, a responsibility which grows as the candidates advance toward Orders or profession. It is scarcely possible that anyone with such a responsibility would accept the decision to admit as sufficient reason for deciding to promote.

It remains no less true today than it was in Gospel times that a vocation is always to a particular mission or office. The Church has more missions and offices to fill than she has apt subjects. It seems that those who make the decisions concerning vocations on behalf of the Church ought to be assured that the candidate not only has general qualifications of virtue and education, but also that the candidate shows as solid a probability as can be established that he or she is qualified to take part in the particular office or mission which a particular community undertakes. I do not know whether teachers are born, and not made; but I do know that if they are not born, they must be made. The admission of candidates who are not suited for the works of a particular institute, whatever other qualities they may possess, can only hinder the vocation of that institute, at least by dissipating its material and human resources.

It is no less true now than it was in Old and New Testament times that God assures the success of a vocation. While the authorities who decide concerning vocations must judge according to prudence, we must not forget that we are not dealing with a merely human problem. They ought to remind themselves regularly that Jean Marie Vianney was an unfit candidate for the priesthod by almost every known standard. We have noticed that the element of unfitness appears in the Bible. God can and does confound the wise and strong by choosing the foolish and the weak. We must also remind ourselves that the use of divine assistance to make up for human weakness is fruitful only through a heroic and total dedication. In one sense no one is worthy of a vocation. No one, whether more or less endowed, can hope to fulfill his vocation without that total commitment which will enable God to work through him. Surely we should be able to encourage candidates to accept the responsibilities with full confidence that they can rise to them.

Finally, we can recall that vocation is still a total commitment demanding renunciation. I am sure that we do not doubt this or think we can make a vocation anything else; I wonder whether we are equally sure that this is the best way to present vocations to the young. Is it entirely in the spirit of the call of Christ to emphasize in vocational programs and literature the presence of swimming pools and picnics, fun and games, new and comfortable buildings in novitiates and seminaries? I remember reading an advertisement placed in the **London Times** by an Antarctic explorer, Sir Robert Scott or Sir Ernest Shackleton; it asked for men who wished to go on an exhausting and dangerous and possibly fatal trip for low pay. When I compare this notice with some of the vocational literature which we see now, it is not difficult to see which invitation more resembles the vocations of the Gospels.

Rudolf Bultmann and The Bible

I. BULTMANN AND 'MYTH'

IT IS NOW twenty-five years since the appearance of Rudolf Bultmann's **Neues Testament und Mythologie** (1941). The controversy over **Entmythologisierung** which has ensued has been called the second major theological event of the century after the appearance of Karl Barth's revised commentary on Romans in 1921. One notable difference between the two events is the degree to which Catholics have engaged in the discussions concerning demythologizing. The neo-orthodoxy of Barth made a very slight impression on Catholics; it did not even reach the entire world of theological scholarship, and students in good seminaries could pursue the study of theology for four years and go on for two more years of graduate work knowing much less about Barth than they did about Pelagius or Molina. Theology in those days was badly in need of an **aggiornamento.** Bultmann has done this for

us if he has done nothing else; a theologian finds
it difficult to maintain indifference towards a figure
who receives complete coverage in **Time.** The contributions of Catholic scholars to the controversy
have been respectfully received by Protestant theologians, including Bultmann himself; I have heard
him quoted — but cannot verify the quotation —
as saying that Rene Marle understands his thoughts
better than any other of his critics. It seems time
to do what the editor of this journal wishes: to re-
view the Catholic reaction to Bultmann and to assess
the effect of Bultmann on Catholic theology. To
do this within the space assigned makes it necessary
that I select the writings of men who can be considered representative.

One is surprised to read that Bultmann may not
have created something really new and original; yet
this is suggested by two of his better critics. L.
Malevez, S.J.,[1] believes that Bultmann has not pushed
the problem of the point of insertion of the supernatural into the natural as far as some Catholic theologians. Malevez mentions only Blondel, but he

---

[1] **Le message chretien et le mythe,** Brussels, 1954, 32; hereafter cited as Malevez.

must have in mind de Lubac and Bouilliard, whose writings on the subject were received inhospitably by perhaps the majority of Catholic theologians. Both of these men published later than Bultmann; had their works received a wider circulation, it is highly probable that Catholic theologians would have been in a better position to assess the work of Bultmann. René Marlé, S.J.,[1] finds that Bultmann has produced a particularly seductive expression of traditional Lutheran doctrine. With the second of these Bultmann himself would agree; it should be noticed that most Lutherans do not think so. A comparison of Bultmann with Catholic work on the problem of the supernatural is difficult because the writers deal with different terms and different approaches. I think myself that Bultmann has gone farther here than Malevez allows.

Bultmann's vague and undefined concept of myth has been under fire from a number of critics, including this writer.[2] It is an open weakness in a posi-

---

[1] **Bultmann et l'interpretation du Noveau Testament,** Paris, 1956, 136; hereafter cited as Marlé.

[2] **Myths and Realities,** Milwaukee, 1963, 266-267; **Malevez,** 64 + 163; Marlé, 62—70; Futrell, **Catholic Biblical Quarterly** 21 (1959), 284-286.

tion which is called "demythologizing" that the idea of myth is left vague. I do not believe that the name is at all apt for what Bultmann wants to do; and a discussion of his work would proceed better if this problem were simply set aside. As it is, Bultmann is vulnerable to criticism which really touches only the fringe of his thesis. This is not to say that his denial of such "myths" as the messianism of Jesus, the virgin birth, the miracles and the resurrection are fringe questions; of course they are not. But confusion is introduced at the outset when these beliefs are lumped as myths with such things as the three-decker universe. Bultmann would say at this point that my use of the word "deny" distorts his thought; it does, but it does not distort the impression his thought has left with many readers, and it is his loose use of the word "myth" which is responsible for the misunderstanding. Bultmann wants to interpret the myth, which supposes that there is a reality expressed by the myth and capable of interpretation. The reader will never guess this from Bultmann's description of myth.

But I have not noticed that Bultmann's critics have

often done anything to remove the confusion about myth; and thus the entire discussion has been unnecessarily fogged in an important area. A large number of recent studies of myth cited in my own paper mentioned above should have been consulted by both Bultmann and his critics. Myth is what Bultmann does not seem to admit that it is, an expression of reality. One should attempt to grasp the pattern of mythical thinking; only then can one hope to interpret the myth.

That Bultmann depends excessively on philosophy is affirmed by several,[3] and Marlé even calls him rigid.[4] The philosophy on which Bultmann depends is the existentialism of the early Heidegger; one of the most curious turns of the entire discussion is that the later Heidegger rejects himself as interpreted by Bultmann. Marlé[1] attacks the existentialist interpretation of the gospel; there is nothing in this system which justifies Bultmann's canonization of it. Bultmann in his own way becomes as dogmatic a philosopher as any other. In Catholic theology we have been aware for some years now — although

---

[3] Malevez 40 ff; Marle, 130-139.   [4] Marlé 149.
[1] 97-104.

the problem has not yet really been opened up —
that the scholasticism which has dominated theology
for several hundred years does not harmonize with
the thought patterns of the Bible. A recent German
symposium[2] assembled contributions from theologians and exegetes. The candor of the discussion
was laudable, and in spite of more finger-wagging
than we need, it marked an advance toward mutual
understanding. The problem faced by exegetes everywhere is the interpretation of the Bible in modern
terms without imposing philosophical categories
upon the Bible. Bultmann has actually surrendered
the exegetical flag; and it is a doubtful advance to
give existentialism the philosophical control which
was formerly exercised by scholasticism. Bultmann
has probably set back Catholic exegetes in their
fumbling towards an **aggiornamento** in philosophy.
How much they fumble can be read in the paper of
Michael Novak.[3]

Bultmann's dependence on philosophy is less annoying than the absolute cult he pays to scientific

---

[2] H. Vorgrimier, **Exegese und Dogmatik,** Mainz, 1962.
[3] **Catholic Biblical Quarterly** 22 (1960), 306-314, with a response by this writer 315-316.

method; not many of his Catholic critics have noticed this, and none of the writers whose criticism is most extensive. Bultmann obviously regards scientific method as the only valid way of thought; and this degrades not only myth but also philosophy. Scientific method is the ultimate canon against which the New Testament is measured; the New Testament, of course, does not meet this canon, but neither does anything else. That scientific method must be under some control does not occur to Bultmann. Theology has enough impediments without adding this one. There is no doubt that we have to meet modern man, but to make this concession is to let modern man determine what we shall tell him; and in that case why bother to meet him at all? Here the remarks of Malevez[4] and Marlé[5] that Bultmann exaggerates the opposition between the Gospels and scientific thought does not meet the problem. The problem is Bultmann's scientism.

History suffers also from Bultmann's existentialism and scientism; the critics have elaborated this in more detail, as I shall point out. More than one writer has remarked that Bultmann dehistoricizes

---

[4] **122 ff.**   [5] **65 ff.**

rather than demythologizes the New Testament.[1]
Marlé[2] and P. J. Cahill[3] have both pointed out this
weakness in Bultmann's thought. The point is subtle.
Bultmann distinguishes between **historisch** and **ge-
schichtlich,** a distinction which is impossible to re-
produce in English; and some of his critics have
failed to grasp the distinction. Even so, the historical Christian event, independently of how one conceives it, is less important in Bultmann's system
than the event which occurs in the believer. It does
not matter much to Bultmann what happened or how
much we can learn about it. The whole program
of demythologizing presupposes that the event must
be detached from its historical roots in order that
it may become actual for the contemporary man.
In all fairness to Bultmann, he is trying to state that
the Christian event is not merely historical but is
an enduring reality. The New Testament has its
own way of stating this. Bultmann may have saved

---

[1] Unfortunately some of this has rubbed off on Form Criticism as a method; the opinion that Form Criticism is anti-
historical by its essence is very widely diffused, and scholars find themselves frequently obliged to explain that anti-
historicism does not rise from Form Criticism but from
philosophical presuppositions.

[2] 9ff. [3] **Theological Studies** 3 (1962), 83.

its enduring reality but lost the historical event on which the enduring reality reposes.

Malevez[4] does not hesitate to summarize Bultmann's thesis as agnosticism. Traditional basic elements of Christianity are not so much removed by Bultmann as ignored. His compendium of the Christian proclamation is as brief and as distorted as Harnack's reduction of the gospel to the fatherhood of God and the brotherhood of man. If Christianity loses all but one or two elements, one can ask whether what is proclaimed is Christianity or a new gospel. Marlé[5] likewise calls demythologizing a subtraction rather than an interpretation. This criticism may over-extend itself. Bultmann should not be judged merely by his articles on demythologizing. His **Theologie des Neuen Testaments**, available in an English translation, is a much fuller statement of biblical belief than one would gather from his article on demythologizing. The book has been vigorously criticized for its interpretations and its omissions — for instance, he depends very little on the Gospels, which means the teaching of Jesus — but it contains some splendid insights into the New Testament. Like

---

[4] 154ff. [5] 68ff.

all of Bultmann's writings, it makes the reader ask questions he never asked before. But it is not at all clear that Bultmann means his theology to be a statement of what the Christian believes; it appears to be rather a synthesis of what the primitive Church believed with no urgency for the modern man. Malevez[6] has noticed that Bultmann is silent about traditional eschatology; one cannot be sure that his search for the meaning of human existence goes beyond this world. Eschatology in Bultmann is never defined except in terms of a finality which is attained now. If the eschatology of the New Testament is a myth, it demands more interpretations than the myth of the three-decker universe. If we learn that heaven and hell are not absolutely up and down, we have learned nothing. If we are told that the concepts are meaningless for human destiny, something has been removed from the gospel which demands a replacement.

II. CHRIST, FAITH, AND THE RESURRECTION

The Christian event, as Bultmann explains it, is "the decisive act of God in Christ." The decisive

---

[6] 157ff.

act consists in this, that one man realized the possibilities of human existence by becoming obedient
unto death, even the death of the cross. The proclamation of the event confronts man with this meaning of existence. Faith is the acceptance of this meaning; and by faith man is saved — that is, man understands the meaning of his existence. This compendium is an unforgivable distortion of Bultmann's
thought; but it seems necessary to state it in the
barest outline in order to discuss the criticism it
has received.

L. Malevez[1] asked whether the event in Bultmann's
theology is subjective or objective. By this Malevez
means that event precisely as the saving event; Bultmann accepts the historical reality of the death of
Jesus by crucifixion, and it is one of the few state-
ments about Jesus which he accepts as historically
verified. But Malevez's question is pointed: does
the event have any value which distinguishes it from
other events? Does its saving character lie in the
event or in my personal response to the event? Is
it the event or the proclamation of the event which
has the power to save? And if salvation consists

---

[1] Malevez, 63 ff.

in understanding the meaning of human existence, is not salvation accomplished entirely within the subject — that is to say, is it not entirely subjective, lacking any objective reality?

Bultmann, I suppose, would say that this question is put in terms of a logic and a metaphysics which he does not accept. By calling it the decisive act of God in Christ he seems to have named something as objective as could be desired. Malevez's question arises from a lack of both clarity and consistency in Bultmann's position. For what precisely did God do **in Christ**? Marle[2] has asked how the cross can be the decisive event unless there be something unique about the person who died on the cross. Bultmann's impoverished Christology haunts him when he speaks of the act of God in Christ; for he has nothing in the event which makes it different from the death of any good man — Socrates, for instance, to whom Jesus has so often been compared. The New Testament, mythological or not, is clear that the saving value of the event rests upon the person in whom God wrought salvation. The New Testament proclaims Christ, not the act of God in Christ:

---

[2] Marle, 150 ff.

for in proclaiming Christ it proclaims the act of God. Without Christology there is no connection between the event and salvation; and how does it remain a saving event? That it should be the occasion of salvation means that something else is the saving event.

This something else can be nothing but the proclamation. Is Christ the saviour in Bultmann's thesis? Malevez[1] and Marlé[2] do not think so. Malevez[3] says that Bultmann has replaced the Lord with the **kerygma**. Christianity has been reduced to preaching.[4] There is nothing left but the word, and it is the word alone which saves. That this eliminates the entire sacramental system is noteworthy enough, although Bultmann is as silent about the sacramental system as he is about eschatology. Sacramentalism in his philosophy would be as mythological as anything in the entire New Testament. But where does the word get the saving power which it must have? The power resides not in the word but in the faith of him who hears the word. Faith is the true agent

---

[1] 74. [2] 182. [3] 121.

[4] Malevez, 152; P. J. Cahill, **Catholic Biblical Quarterly** 24 (1962), 303-304.

of salvation — which gives a peculiar pungency to the words of Paul that we are saved by faith and not by works. This means ultimately that the believer is the agent of his own salvation.

From where does the word come in Bultmann's thesis? As Marlé has pointed out,[5] there is no place for the Church in Bultmann's scheme. The proclamation seems to hang in the air as a kind of detached and disembodied shape, as a sound with no speaker to utter it. If Christ is not really the saviour, then there can really be no Church. As the New Testament conceives the Church, it becomes altogether superfluous; what is there left for the Church to do? It has no sacramental function, and it has no witness to bear. Here appears another weakness in the existential encounter of Bultmann: the social character of the Church is lost. Individual piety becomes dominant. There is a long tradition of individualistic piety in both Catholicism and Protestantism in which the place of the individual person is exaggerated. Recent theological thinking has begun to see more clearly the Church as a body; Bultmann moves in the opposite direction, and it is a

5   159.

backward movement. The atomizing of the Church can scarcely be a sound attempt to make the gospel more appealing to modern man, who is more and more alienated and isolated from his society. In Bultmann's gospel one finds nothing of the ideal of the unity of all men in Christ.

It may be pressing the point too far, but that is a risk I shall have to run; and I submit that the existentialist philosophy in its search for the meaning of existence in an affirmation of self is just the self-centered philosophy which is in opposition to the basic teaching of the gospel that one must lose one's self to find one's self. Bultmann is too good an exegete to be unaware of this; the meaning of existence lies in obedience even unto the death of the cross. But I believe that the philosophical categories in which he has chosen to interpret the message are too directly in opposition to the message itself to become its vehicle. The self in the gospel finds its fulfillment only in relation to other selves; for the self is made perfect by the commandment of love. This element has not received its due attention in Bultmann's interpretation, if indeed it has received any attention.

The failure of Bultmann to present salvation in any terms which correspond to the thought of the New Testament is largely due to his refusal to accept the Old Testament as a necessary presupposition to the proclamation. In a recent symposium on Bultmann and the Old Testament[1] this writer suggested that it is only the history of Israel which isolates Jesus Christ from other saviour figures who could be thought to resemble him — culture heroes, king-saviours, cosmic men, mythological bearers of life. To these there correspond in the modern world political saviours, economic prophets, scientific sages, military heroes, psychotherapist bearers of life. Jesus is none of these; but it is only as the saviour of Israel that he can be recognized in his true character. It is as Messiah that the New Testament understood him and proclaimed him, and if one dismisses this as mythological one inevitably turns Jesus into some kind of secular saviour. Bultmann has not surely done this; but he may have avoided it by taking away from Jesus any genuine saving function.

[1] B. W. Anderson, **The Old Testament and Christian Faith,** New York, 1963, 108-109.

There is yet another and quite serious lack of concord between Bultmann's thesis and the New Testament. There is no doubt that the cross is central in the proclamation; it was scandal to the Jews and folly to the Greeks, and Paul himself said that he proclaimed Christ and Him crucified. But it is impossible to separate the cross from the resurrection in the New Testament.[2] Jesus saves through his death and his resurrection. Christian theology has not always perceived this; and in assured orthodox theological traditions there has at times been no exposition of the resurrection as a part of the saving event. In recent apologetics the resurrection has been most frequently considered as a proof of the messianic character and of the divinity of Jesus; this emphasis does not repose on the New Testament. Bultmann could be easily excused in this matter for not going beyond so many of his predecessors. His problem is that he has made it impossible for himself to go beyond them. The resurrection is an outstanding example of the mythological. However Bultmann interprets it, the resurrection cannot be interpreted as an event; and it is only

---

[2] Marlé, 162 ff.

as an event that it has saving value. In the New Testament it is the resurrection which raises the cross above the level of the merely historical event which is commemorated. Without the resurrection the cross cannot be the decisive act of God in Christ.

Demythologizing the New Testament means that the events of the New Testament are reduced to a scanty historical kernel. It means further that when they are considered as significant, they are detached from their background in the history of Israel and from the reality of the history and the culture of Palestine of the first century. It is just this historical involvement, Bultmann thinks, which makes them irrelevant to modern man. The New Testament is dated and therefore meaningless. But take the act of God in Christ out of the obscurity of history and culture and let it appear in its luminous purity, and it will reveal the meaning of human existence. This is obviously a program of preaching, not of scholarship. The office of the scholar is to understand the New Testament so that he can isolate the proclamation from the mythology in which it is embedded. One must ask whether his study of the mythological encasement will really make the proclamation more intelligible to him; but that is not the question which first rises here.

The question is whether the gospel has not been converted into a philosophy. The gospel is revelation, and philosophy is thought; this distinction will stand no matter how one takes the terms "revelation" and "thought." Does Bultmann's existentialist statement of the saving event need the revelation of the gospel? And what is it that is revealed? The proclamation seems to be no more than the occasion from which a philosophical insight rises. It is not surely, it seems, a necessary occasion. Bultmann may have revived a modern form of Christian **gnosis**. The great Alexandrian Origen was the first Christian thinker to attempt a systematic expression of Christian belief in philosophical terms. The system had tremendous influence, in spite of the fact that it was not really successful. It is an interesting parallel that Origen found it difficult to incorporate the saving events of the death and resurrection into his system. The goal of the system was insight; and this is the goal of Bultmann. But insight is not salva-

tion. P. Benoit[1] notices that Bultmann is an idealist; he rejects the body. This idealism Bultmann
has in common with Origen, whose philosophy was
Platonic. The idealist thinker cannot assimilate
death and resurrection as saving events; they do
not fit the categories of his thought.

Thus the search for the meaning of human existence seems to break down, because it does not arrive
at an understanding of what man is; at least its understanding of man is not the understanding of the
New Testament. In the gospel it is the whole man
who is under judgment and who is saved. His sin
is not the incarnation of his soul, and his salvation
is not liberation from his body. It is the beginning
of a new life in the risen Christ, who is a whole man.
One must accept man as he is before he can accept
God. Obscurity in the understanding of the meaning of human existence may on analysis turn out
to be nothing more than a refusal to recognize the
human condition. If this is not recognized, one will
scarcely feel the need for salvation from it.

---

[1] **Exegese et theologie I,** Paris, 1961, 62.

III. DEBT TO BULTMANN

In the preceding parts of this survey I have mentioned some of the major criticisms of the thought of Rudolf Bultmann which have been written by Catholics. The criticisms were selected because I thought they exposed genuine and deep differences between Bultmann and Catholic theological thinking — in so far as Catholic theological thinking can be taken as a single whole. When the differences are enumerated as I have done here, one can be somewhat surprised to learn that Bultmann's critics are usually sympathetic, even friendly. Catholics have criticized each other with more rancor than they exhibit towards Bultmann, who in the popular mind is as far out as one can get. We cannot survey this work without noticing that Bultmann's critics do not treat him as being that far out. They respect him because of some positive values in his work.

The first of these values is Bultmann's learning. Disputes with Bultmann do not arise from his ignorance. His works are not written for beginners, and beginners are not advised to read them; beginners lack the information and critical training to read them with profit. But no New Testament scholar now would deny his indebtedness to Bultmann's erudition and understanding. Whatever he proposes is based on knowledge which few scholars of his generation can equal, and he must be taken seriously. One learns from Bultmann even when one disagrees with him.

One recognizes in Bultmann a scholar of transparent honesty and a deep religious faith. Sincerity, of course, is not enough for scholarship; but when it is present it lends weight. One feels slightly unhappy when critics of Bultmann attack his personal integrity or his religiosity, especially when the critics are members of one's own church. Bultmann is ready to submit his opinions to discussion and criticism; and this is more than I can say for some of his critics — adding that this remark refers to none of the writers whom I have mentioned in this survey. One who engages in a critique of Bultmann's writings learns that he must take faith seriously; and this is a lesson which the theologian cannot repeat too often.

A survey of Bultmann's views such as I have undertaken here, and even the longer works which I have quoted, often fails to do justice to his views. His thought is subtle and not readily subject to summarization. We critics are more frequently drawing what we believe are inevitable consequences from his views; Bultmann vigorously denies that such arguments are logically consequent, and perhaps we ought to charge him with inconsistency rather than unorthodoxy. But this charge will not stick easily either. John Macquarrie compared the study of Bultmann to a ride in a wildly-piloted vehicle, which is always on the edge of the precipice but averted at the last instant when a plunge seems certain. Macquarrie is sympathetic; many critics, especially Catholics, would say that the vehicle is already a heap of wreckage at the bottom of the canyon. Evidently this too is exaggerated; a discussion which is sustained for over twenty-five years is unlikely to continue over a dead issue. Bultmann does not depart as far from orthodoxy as summaries like this must suggest; and his position has more strength than I have been able to give it here. It cannot be dismissed **en bloc**; and this is what makes it annoying. One could — not without a slight degree of impudence — designate the controversy as the demythologizing of Bultmann.

Personally I have found the greatest value in Bultmann's writings to be his genius for asking the right questions. I reject his answers more frequently than I accept them, but I confess that I would not have asked the questions if Bultmann had not; and therefore I would not have answered them. It would not be candid to claim that my formulation of the answers is entirely free of the influence of Bultmann's answers. I suggest that there are very few contemporary biblical interpreters — and none of any stature — who have not adopted something of Bultmann's approach and methods. If we deal with the problems he raises, we find that we cannot deal with them in the tired old methods of past generations. We think like Bultmann in order to reach conclusions other than the conclusions of Bultmann. This can be seen even in men who are not familiar with his writings; they have absorbed more than they know, because there is so much of Bultmann in the air.

What are some of the questions which he raises? The first is without doubt the problem of the relevance of the gospel to "modern man." "Modern man" is in a certain sense a fiction of reason of the type which the careful historian avoids; but here the fiction represents reality. Bultmann has opened the cupboard in which some of our skeletons are kept, and he has made it impossible to maintain some pretences. The Catholic Church is well aware that it has almost no influence at all on the intellectual classes of Europe and America. To say this is to impute no blame; but the Church is not served by denying the fact. I think she is not served by denying that there are enough of the hierarchy and the clergy who project a clear image of thought control as their ideal of the Church. The unbelieving intellectual is repelled by this image; and believing intellectuals, who are also repelled by it, have not until very recently made themselves heard in any volume on this subject.

By facing this problem Bultmann has compelled us to ask ourselves what we are doing about it; and if we are sure that he is not doing it the right way,

LIBRARY ST. MARY'S COLLEGE

we ought in decency to propose what we think is the right way. The Church is for all, learned and unlearned alike; but it is a strange idea of the Church by which one would think that it can appeal to the intellectual by being frankly, even brutally anti-intellectual. Bultmann has sketched a faith for the intellectual. Catholics do not believe that there is one faith for the intellectual and another for the un-learned; but they believe that the one faith is apt for both. It is not that we need to make our presen-tation suit the demands of the intellectual, but only that we remove those elements foreign to the faith which make him think sincerely that the Church does not permit thought unless it is hierarchically controlled.

Bultmann is in danger, as his critics have noted, of substituting a philosophy for faith; and indeed this is historically the danger of the believing intel-lectual. If this is the danger which Bultmann incurs, we do not avoid the danger merely by criticizing the existentialist philosophy in which he interprets the proclamation. The issue is not whether this philosophy or that should be substituted for faith,

148

but whether any philosophy should be substituted for faith. I think Catholics have as much reason to ask this question as anyone else. Bultmann is the heir of a theological tradition which is sometimes called Lutheran scholasticism. He is a rebellious heir, but it has influenced him deeply. He sees in his own theological traditions an antiquated metaphysics which ignores all thought since the seventeenth century and sits contemplating its own navel. It makes him impatient. I have no quarrel with his impatience, but only with his conviction that he must replace the antiquated metaphysics with another metaphysics which will do the same thing. But we should be grateful that he has submitted the metaphysics to a vigorous and unsparing theological criticism, by which I mean a criticism based on theological sources. We are quick to submit his own metaphysics to this type of criticism; we shall prove our candor when we submit our own metaphysics to criticism. There is room for some demythologizing here.

I said in an earlier part of this survey that Bultmann's interpretation of the message exaggerates the place of the individual person to the point where he nearly atomizes the Church as a society. This criticism has to be modified, although it remains valid. Bultmann's presentation of the **kerygma** as encounter which issues in commitment has made a deep impression on contemporary theology; and this is one of the finest fruits of his work. Permit me to illustrate. I do not know whether British readers are familiar with a minor sociological classic written by William Whyte, published in the United States a few years ago under the title of **The Organization Man.** This was a serious study of the effects of the large corporation on the personal psychology, the family life, the economic habits and the morals of its executives. The book was frightening; readers of George Orwell's **1984** found too many echoes. The difference was that Mr. Whyte did not deal with government, nor was his account fictional. The erosion of the individual person has gone much farther than we think; and this occurs on those economic and social levels where we think the individual person has more liberty to affirm himself.

To the Catholic the book was even more frightening because so much of this capitalistic collectivism reminded him sharply of what he had observed in the Church. To put it in a word, the Catholic was reminded that to many of his fellow Catholics membership in the Church is sufficient; it gives them the security which they want. They have never thought of the Church as a personal encounter with God which demands a personal decision. They are Catholics because they have never decided to be anything else. But a personal decision they do not want, and many of their clergy would discourage them if they did want it. It is widely agreed that membership equips one with a complete set of prefabricated moral decisions which will see one through any moral crisis, including the defense of one's bomb shelter.

There seems to be ample room to incorporate some of the elements of encounter and commitment in our own form of the proclamation. If we do, we shall give these elements a much larger dimension than Bultmann was able to give them. For the Church is the living Christ, the enduring reality of the saving event. We confront the event itself, and we are more aware of the urgency of the encounter. To think of the Church as a mere organization obscures the enduring reality. We are also more aware of the depth of the commitment. Bultmann's faith, as his critics notice, remains substantially the primitive Lutheran faith which fails to reveal the possibilities of the new life in Christ. The Church discloses to her members what the commitment engages them to. They are doers of the word, and not hearers only. We have actually not had enough emphasis on either hearing or doing, but particularly on doing. Many of our Catholic people think of themselves as objects rather than as subjects of the action of the Church; and an object does not feel a deep sense of commitment.

This survey has attempted to show some of the reasons why the thought of Rudolf Bultmann is so important to our generation. I am aware that it is not eminently successful. The task is too large for a limited space; and an examination of his thought demands a background for which there has been no room. But a man who has become almost a household word deserves at least this much attention.

The Language of The Old Testament

WHEN WE turn our attention to the liturgical language of the Old Testament, we must recall that there is hardly any history of the Hebrew language. The text of the Old Testament was submitted to a constant process of retouching and modernization up to the last centuries before the Christian era, and this process has destroyed most of the evidence of development. Our modern Hebrew Bible exhibits surprising homogeneity in grammar, vocabulary, structure, and idiom from the earliest books of the Old Testament to the latest, which are separated from each other by nearly a thousand years, roughly the period which separates modern English from **Beowulf**. This homogeneity makes the language of the Bible by itself an unreliable criterion for dating the books of the Bible. Here and there a few evident signs of a later stage of the language are scattered, but we do not know enough about the language to take these signs as

155

sufficient evidence by themselves. Archaisms also are found, but these can be deliberately employed as literary ornamentation, especially in poetry. This condition of the Hebrew language is itself a sign of how the Hebrews treated the Old Testament books when Hebrew was still a living language.

Old Testament history is divided into the pre-exilic period (before 587 B.C.) and the exilic and post-exilic periods (from 587 B.C. to the beginning of the Christian era). In the pre-exilic period there is no evidence whatever of the existence of a sacred liturgical language. Indeed, no sacred liturgical language appears anywhere in the ancient Near East. In Mesopotamia, for instance, liturgical texts are often archaic in style; but when liturgical texts had been composed in Sumerian, they were translated into Akkadian. Some passages of the Old Testament are certainly liturgical passages, and the language of these passages does not differ from the language of the narrative, rhetorical and poetic portions of the Old Testament. It is a safe assumption that the language of the pre-exilic cult was the common vernacular language.

THE LANGUAGE OF THE OLD TESTAMENT

The destruction of the Hebrew kingdoms by the Assyrians and the Babylonians in the eighth and sixth centuries B.C. brought many revolutionary changes in Hebrew life and institutions. One of these changes was the spread of Aramaic, the common language of the Near East, to the point where Hebrew ceased to exist as a living language during the post-exilic period. The change was gradual, not sudden; there are a number of books and passages of the Old Testament written in Hebrew during these four centuries. But by the last pre-Christian century, if not earlier, Hebrew was no longer employed as a common medium of communication.

The question of the language of the Old Testament and of Hebrew worship did not arise until the spread of Aramaic as the common language. The question became more acute with the conquest of the East by Alexander and the diffusion of Jewish communities through the Greek-speaking world. The preservation of the text of the Old Testament after the abandonment of Hebrew was the work of the schools of the rabbis. It is impossible to date precisely the beginning of the rabbinical schools and their work on the Old Testament and the preservation of their traditions. It is certain that these schools existed in New Testament times; and some passages of Ben Sira (39:1ff) show that the rabbinical conception of the Law and the scribe existed in the early second century B.C. Ezra, who probably lived in the fourth century B.C., has been called the father of the rabbinical schools. This designation may exaggerate his importance; but the foundation of rabbinical schools should probably be put in the fourth or third century B.C. With these schools the formation of Judaism began.

How carefully the rabbis preserved the text of the Old Testament during this early period it is impossible to determine, nor do we know how much freedom they allowed themselves in editing the text. The Isaiah MSS. of Qumran exhibit a Hebrew text closely identical with the text of the earliest MS. previously known, which comes from the ninth century A.D. This indicates that greater care was exercised in preserving the text during the early period than scholars had commonly believed. The early rabbis, however, did not show the fanatical fidelity to the traditional text which was shown by the rabbis of the second or third century A.D. and later. The attitude of the rabbis toward the text is connected with the question of when the books of the Old Testament came to be regarded by the Jews precisely as sacred books, the text of which may not be altered by any human authority. The date of the origin of this conception cannot be given exactly; but it was certainly earlier than the New Testament period.

Hebrew continued in use in the rabbinical schools after it had ceased to be a common medium of communication. The Hebrew employed by the rabbis was not the same as the language of the Old Testament, and the rabbis were aware of the difference. They distiguished biblical Hebrew as "the language of the Bible" from their own Hebrew, "the language of scholars." Rabbinical Hebrew may be compared to the Latin of the medieval scholastic theology; it was a technical language, restricted to the schools and to certain learned disciplines.

The problem of making the Bible and the liturgical formulae intelligible to congregations of the synagogues was at first solved in the most practical way. The Hebrew text of the Bible was read in the synagogue, but it was accompanied by a translation into Aramaic made orally, either by verses or by sections. Custom prohibited the translator from having any manuscript before him; but early in the formation of Judaism written translations called targums appeared which the translator could study in private before he performed his function in public. A number of these translations have been preserved; they show a surprising freedom in the interpretation of the text of the Bible. At this period the rabbis felt no scruple in expanding the text of the Bible by the addition of extraneous material or in interpreting it in a sense quite other than the sense which the words bear. For instance, the targum of the suffering servant of Isaias 53 removes from the passage the idea of suffering and death. The reading was followed by a discourse, also in Aramaic. Such a synagogue service is mentioned in the Gospel accounts of the appearance of Jesus in the synagogue of Nazareth. The prayers also were uttered in Aramaic, often interspersed with phrases of biblical Hebrew.

THE LANGUAGE OF THE OLD TESTAMENT

In the Greek-speaking communities outside Palestine Greek was employed, and the translation of the Old Testament called the Septuagint was made for the Jews of Egypt in the second or first century B.C. In the Greek synagogues Greek was very probably also the language of prayer. This development was reversed somewhat by the Maccabean wars of the second century B.C. The attempt of Antiochus Epiphanes to Hellenize the Jews was met by a resistance which focused on all the identifying features of Judaism, and this included the use of Hebrew. In Palestine the use of Greek as a language of the Bible and of prayer was largely abandoned, although its use was continued in Jewish communities elsewhere. From this period probably comes the precept of rabbinical tradition that the father must teach his son Hebrew. But during the classical period of rabbinical Judaism, which extended into the third century A.D., prayers could be recited in any language; in the synagogue the priestly blessing had to be recited in Hebrew. It was probably not before the second century A.D. that Hebrew began to be regarded with almost superstitious reverence;

it was called the sacred language. It became the only acceptable language of prayer in the synagogue; and in the opinion of some rabbis the interceding angels, who present men's prayers to God, speak only Hebrew and cannot understand prayer uttered in Aramaic. But this exaggerated reverence for Hebrew was accompanied by a sincere and thorough effort to give every Jew a sufficient knowledge of Hebrew to enable him to follow the readings and prayers of the synagogue. To the same end prayers acquired fixed formulae, although prayer books with written formulae were a creation of the medieval period.

This brief sketch shows how Judaism met the challenge of changing historical and cultural conditions. As far as the religious life of the individual Jew was concerned, the solution must be judged successful. Not every Jew was well acquainted with the Old Testament and the ritual of the synagogue; the Gospels refer to the multitude which knows not the Law and is accursed. But in Judaism both early and late, especially after the Jews became a segregated society, the Jews as a group were familiar with the text of the Bible and with the liturgy of the synagogue. At no time was the language a barrier between themselves and their worship. If here and there a barrier arose, it was soon broken down by the ingenuity of the rabbis; in one period they were ready to translate the sacred books and the ritual into the vernacular, in another period to preserve the sacred language by undertaking a program of mass education. The preservation of the language was a part of their resistance to assimilation by a much larger and extremely active gentile culture. Had the rabbis not feared this assimilation, it seems doubtful that in the normal course of events they could have abandoned the vernacular. By retaining Hebrew they helped to retain that peculiar union of religion and nationalism which has been the mark of Judaism since the beginning of the Christian era.

A glance at primitive Christian practice will help to illustrate our subject. The primitive Christian community was at first Jewish, and the scheme of their liturgical worship with its prayers and reading was the scheme of the synagogue. There is no doubt that the liturgy of the first Palestinian Christian communities was conducted in Aramaic, the language of the country. It is equally certain that the liturgical language of the first Greek-speaking communities was Greek from their foundation. As long as Greek remained the common language of the Mediterranean world, it remained the language of the liturgy; Latin was not introduced except in those parts of the Roman world where Latin was spoken, and these were isolated areas in the West. The use of Latin in the liturgy grew with the vernacular use of Latin, and it became the predominant liturgical language only when the Greek churches seceded in a body from the See of Rome. By this time Latin also had become a dead language.

It is not my purpose to trace the development of Lat:n as a liturgical language, except for purposes of comparison. Hebrew as a liturgical language first appears in Judaism. We must admit that the rabbis were alive to the fact that language, even when it is a liturgical language, is a means of communication. When the problem first arose, the traditional language was abandoned without hesitation in public worship. The reasons for ultimately retaining the traditional language had nothing to do with the liturgy; they arose from the desire of a group to resist assimilation and to preserve its identity as a unit which was national and cultural as well as religious. The effort was successful, but it had its price. The group preserved itself by building a wall which cut off communication with the non-Jewish world. As a dynamic religious force Judaism had no effect on the outside world. But within the group the education of its members in the liturgical language was undertaken with great pains and with astonishing success; we may judge both if we imagine the magnitude of the task of teaching Latin to all Catholics of the Roman Rite. The Latin Church has not even undertaken this task; it is doubtful whether the task could be successfully accomplished or whether it would be worth the effort. Hence one fact stands out in a comparison of the two liturgical languages: Hebrew has long been generally understood by Jews, and Latin is not generally understood by Latin Catholics. It does not fall within the scope of this paper to analyze the causes of this condition or to point out what may be done to change it. But I believe that it does fall within the scope of this paper to point out that the condition exists.

Language exists purely as a means of communication and for no other reason. Latin is no more a sacred tongue than Hebrew. The rabbis may have thought that Hebrew was the language of the interceding angels; but Catholics, I trust, do not think that God understands Latin any better than he understands English, German, or Swahili. St. Paul, who was a rabbi as well as an apostle, set no great store by the ability to speak foreign languages; if he sings with his tongue, he prefers to sing also with his intelligence. Public worship, as distinguished from private worship, exists because man is a social being, and it is intended to unite the members of the group as well as to give glory to God. It is difficult to understand how the members of the group communicate with God and with each other in social worship when their social prayer is recited by a solitary representative in a language unknown to them. The history of Judaism shows us that it is

THE LANGUAGE OF THE OLD TESTAMENT

possible to preserve a sacred language; it also shows us that it was done at the cost of dynamism and universal appeal. The Church, it is true, possesses an inner dynamism which no human device can suppress; but the contrast between the Judaism of the first century and Christianity of the first century in this respect offers material for serious reflection. What is the oldest tradition in the Church concerning liturgical language?

THE FAITH

of the

CATHOLIC CHURCH

BY F. VAN der MEER

Here is the first new explanation of the Catholic Creed published in America since the conclusion of the Vatican Council: **a complete, up-to-date and popular guide to the whole body of Catholic beliefs and practices contained in the Creed,** more than 600 pages of detailed information on all phrases and terms which form the substance of the Catholic Faith.

This is the finest one-volume guide you can obtain today to Catholic belief and practice. In it you will find a steady reliance on the teachings of the Bible, the Fathers and Doctors as well as major teachers of the Faith from Augustine to Newman, and the most important exponents of current theology.

The Faith of the Catholic Church is a home reference volume designed for easy use by laymen, an authoritative teaching resource for priests and religious, an encyclopedia of Catholic belief of indispensable importance to secular as well as Catholic libraries.

NEW BOOKS — SPRING 1967

Quantity

.... John L. McKenzie, S. J.	VITAL CONCEPTS OF THE BIBLE	$4.50
.... Adrian van Kaam, C.S. Sp.	PERSONALITY FULFILLMENT IN THE RELIGIOUS LIFE Volume 1:	$5.95
.... Harold Waters	CHRIST OVER THE SEVEN SEAS	$5.95
.... Sr. Mary Immaculate, C.S.C.	GOD LIVES: Great Literature on the World and Its Maker:	$6.00
.... Hilda Lazaron, Ph.D.	SIX CENTURIES OF FRENCH LITERATURE	$9.95
.... Shane Leslie	LONG SHADOWS	$6.95

PUBLICATIONS OF 1966

.... John L. McKenzie, S. J.	MASTERING THE MEANING OF THE BIBLE	$3.50
.... Adrian van Kaam, C.S. Sp.	ART OF EXISTENTIAL COUNSELING	$4.50
.... Adrian van Kaam, C.S. Sp.	PERSONALITY FULFILLMENT IN THE SPIRITUAL LIFE	$3.95
.... F. VanderMeer	FAITH OF THE CATHOLIC CHURCH	$9.95
.... A. Guillerand	PRAYER OF PRESENCE OF GOD	$3.95
.... Dom I. Ryelandt, O.S.B.	UNION WITH CHRIST	$3.95
.... William Smoldon, Ph.D.	A HISTORY OF MUSIC	$9.95
.... John Lynch	THIS LITTLE WHILE (A Life of Christ)	$3.75
....	THE ENCYCLOPEDIA OF CATHOLIC SAINTS (12 vols.)	$59.95

BACKLIST BEST-SELLERS

.... Teilhard de Chardin	BUILDING THE EARTH	$3.50
	DeLuxe Edition (Slipcase)	$5.00
.... Albert Nevins, N. M.	THE MARYKNOLL CATHOLIC DICTIONARY	$9.95
.... Philip Hughes	CATHOLIC FAITH IN PRACTICE	$5.95
.... Mark Tierney	THE COUNCIL AND THE MASS	$3.50
.... J. Roche, S. J.	THE BLESSED VIRGIN'S SILENCE	$3.00
.... Francois Mauriac	ANGUISH AND JOY OF THE CHRISTIAN LIFE	$2.95
.... Father Francois	THE SIMPLE STEPS TO GOD	$3.50
.... Sister Madeleva, C.S.C.	A CHILD ASKS FOR A STAR (Christmas Poems)	$3.50
.... R. L. Bruckberger	SECRET WAYS OF PRAYER	$2.95
.... Martin D'Arcy, S. J.	OF GOD AND MAN	$3.95
.... Bernard Kelly, C.S. Sp.	THY KINGDOM COME	$4.50
.... Dom I. Ryelandt, O.S.B.	THE LIFE OF GRACE	$3.50
.... E. Rhynd	SPIRITUAL TEACHINGS OF THE CHURCH	$5.95
.... D. Mould	ST. BRIGID	$3.00
.... A. Guillerand	WHERE SILENCE IS PRAISE	$2.95
.... Dom I. Ryelandt, O.S.B.	MASS AND THE INTERIOR LIFE	$2.75
.... B. Capelle, O.S.B.	A NEW LIGHT ON THE MASS	$2.95
.... George Shuster	WORLD'S GREAT CATHOLIC LITERATURE	$6.95